NEW TESTAMENT GREEK GRAMMAR

Key to Exercises

NEW TESTAMENT GREEK GRAMMAR

Key to Exercises

MOLLY WHITTAKER

SCM PRESS LTD

334 00830 1

First published 1969
by SCM Press Ltd
56 Bloomsbury Street London WC1
Third impression 1980

Printed in Great Britain by
Fletcher & Son Ltd, Norwich

NOTE

Brackets enclose alternatives or synonyms or optional extras. *Or* has been used when a word admits of two rather different meanings, either of which would be possible in the context of short sentences.

CHAPTER 1

NB The first six verbs cover all the persons and the alternative translations (e.g. λύω *I loose, am loosing, do loose*) are given. After this it is assumed that the student does not need to be assured of the correctness of these alternatives, but they will sometimes be introduced in the following exercises as a reminder of their existence.

They see (are seeing, do see). You (ye) send (are sending, do send). We eat (are eating, do eat). He (she, it) saves (is saving, does save). Thou (you sing.) hearest (art hearing, dost hear). I find (am finding, do find). You (ye) heal. You (sing.) write. They say. We take *or* receive. He (she, it) believes (trusts). You (pl.) proclaim *or* preach. They loose.

λέγομεν, ἀκούει, πιστεύουσι(ν), θεραπεύεις, λαμβάνω, γράφουσι(ν), πέμπετε, εὑρίσκει, σώζομεν, κηρύσσεις, ἐσθίω, βλέπετε, λύομεν.

CHAPTER 2

1. The slave eats the bread of God (God's bread). 2. The angels *or* messengers save the brothers. 3. You (pl.) write the brothers' words (words of the brothers) to *or* for the slaves. 4. O brother, you believe (trust) in the angels' *or* messengers' words (words of the angels *or* messengers). 5. The brother sends the boat. 6. The children take *or* receive the money of the slaves (the slaves' money). 7. The brother is writing the gospel to *or* for the slaves. 8. The demons (devils) take *or* receive the child's cloak (cloak of the child). 9. We preach *or* proclaim the gospel.

1. βλέπομεν τὰ ἔργα τοῦ Θεοῦ. 2. εὑρίσκουσι(ν) οἱ ἀδελφοὶ τὰ εὐαγγέλια. 3. ὦ ἄγγελε, γράφεις τοὺς λόγους τοῦ εὐαγγελίου τοῖς τέκνοις. 4. λαμβάνουσι(ν) (λαμβάνει) τὰ τέκνα τοῦ Θεοῦ τὸ εὐαγγέλιον. 5. σώζει τὰ ἱμάτια τοῖς ἀδελφοῖς.

6. πέμπουσι(ν) οἱ δοῦλοι τὰ πλοῖα. 7. ἐσθίουσι(ν) (ἐσθίει) τὰ δαιμόνια τὸν ἄρτον τῶν τέκνων. 8. ἀκούω τοὺς λόγους τοῦ νόμου.

CHAPTER 3

1. The slaves are leading the apostles into the house. 2. The Lord keeps and saves the world. 3. You (pl.) do not bear witness to the gospel, (O) brother. 4. The apostle calls the demons (devils) out of the children. 5. We are seeking (for) the money in the house. 6. You make loaves for the master, (O) slaves. 7. The angels or messengers speak the words of God (God's words). 8. The children ask (for) bread. 9. (O) Lord, you save the brothers from death. 10. We do not find the clothes in the slave's house (house of the slave).

1. μαρτυρεῖ ὁ νόμος τοῖς λόγοις τοῦ Θεοῦ. 2. κρύπτομεν τὸν ἄρτον ἐν τῷ οἴκῳ. 3. γράφουσι(ν) οἱ ἀπόστολοι εὐαγγέλια τῷ κόσμῳ. 4. λαμβάνεις τὰ ἱμάτια τοῦ τέκνου ἐκ τοῦ οἴκου. 5. καλεῖτε τὸ τέκνον τοῦ δούλου. 6. οὐχ εὑρίσκουσι(ν) (εὑρίσκει) τὰ δαιμόνια τὸ ἀργύριον τῶν τέκνων. 7. τελεῖ τὸ ἔργον τοῦ ἀποστόλου. 8. αἰτοῦσι(ν) οἱ ἄγγελοι ἄρτους. 9. πιστεύουσι(ν) οἱ ἀδελφοὶ (ἐν) τῷ νόμῳ (εἰς τὸν νόμον) τοῦ Κυρίου. 10. ἀκούει καὶ τηρεῖ ὁ κύριος τὸν λόγον τοῦ Θεοῦ.

CHAPTER 4

1. Therefore the brothers are seeking (for) the kingdom of God; for they love (the) truth. 2. How do you (sing.) speak the words of the gospel in the church on the sabbath, but do not keep (observe) the commandments? 3. We do the works of the law, but we believe (trust) in the gospel; for in the words of the apostles we find (the) truth. 4. The angel saves men (mankind) from sin, but the demons (devils) lead to death; for they have authority in the world. 5. The slaves do the works (i.e. they work)

on the sea (lake), but the master takes *or* receives and keeps the money for the children.

NB In translating into Greek there is often little to choose between ἀλλά and δέ, except that the former is found less often and gives greater emphasis. In consecutive prose δέ is often an introductory particle, linking a sentence to the preceding one, and as such is commonly not translated into English.

1. εὑρίσκετε τὴν ἀγάπην καὶ τὴν εἰρήνην ἐν τῇ ἐκκλησίᾳ· πιστεύουσι(ν) γὰρ οἱ ἀδελφοὶ (ἐν) τοῖς λόγοις (εἰς τοὺς λόγους) τοῦ Κυρίου. 2. ζητοῦμεν οὖν τὴν δικαιοσύνην ἐν ταῖς ἐντολαῖς τοῦ νόμου, ὁ δὲ νόμος οὐ σώζει ἐκ τῆς ἁμαρτίας. 3. ποιεῖ ὁ Θεὸς (τὰ) σημεῖα τῷ κόσμῳ, πιστεύουσι(ν) δὲ οἱ ἄνθρωποι (ἐν) τοῖς δαιμονίοις (εἰς τὰ δαιμόνια)· ἄγει γὰρ ἡ ἁμαρτία καὶ τοὺς ἀδελφοὺς εἰς τὸν θάνατον. 4. λαλοῦσι(ν) (λαλεῖ) οὖν τὰ τέκνα τῷ ἀποστόλῳ ἐν τῷ ἱερῷ· φιλεῖ γὰρ τὰ τέκνα, ἀλλ᾽ ἐν τοῖς ἀνθρώποις βλέπει τὰς ἁμαρτίας τοῦ κόσμου. 5. ὦ ἀδελφέ, αἰτεῖς ἄρτους, ἀλλ᾽ ἐσθίομεν τὸν ἄρτον τῶν ἀγγέλων, οὐ τῶν ἀνθρώπων. 6. πῶς ποιεῖς τὰ ἔργα τοῦ Θεοῦ ἐν τῷ σαββάτῳ;

NB Greek semicolons have sometimes been introduced to replace English commas and vice versa, but this is a matter of choice.

CHAPTER 5

1. The young men are building the temple with the prophet's slaves (the slaves of the prophet), but the Lord does not ask (for) a house. 2. The girl has a disease, but the son of man heals diseases. 3. O master, you do not hear the words of the tongue, but you see the works of men. 4. The baptist loves righteousness and proclaims in the desert the kingdom of God; therefore we keep (observe) the prophet's commandments (commandments of the prophet). 5. O disciples, you receive *or* take authority in the village, but the apostles bear witness to the world. 6. O young man, I am talking to the girls before the temple; for they seek peace and truth from the gospel.

5

1. ἄγουσι(ν) οἱ δοῦλοι τὰς παρθένους ἐκ τοῦ οἴκου εἰς τὴν κώμην, ὁ δὲ οἰκοδεσπότης τηρεῖ τὰ τέκνα σὺν τοῖς νεανίαις πρὸ τοῦ ἱεροῦ. 2. ἐν (δὲ) τῇ ἐκκλησίᾳ βλέπομεν τὴν δόξαν τοῦ Θεοῦ· μαρτυροῦσι(ν) γὰρ οἱ ἀδελφοὶ τῇ δικαιοσύνῃ καὶ τῇ ἀληθείᾳ. 3. καλεῖτε τοὺς νεανίας ἐκ τῶν πλοίων πρὸ τοῦ σαββάτου· αἰτοῦσι(ν) οὖν ἄρτον τοῖς τέκνοις. 4. ὦ Κύριε, σώζεις τὸν κόσμον καὶ τοὺς ἀνθρώπους ἐκ (ἀπὸ) τῆς ἐξουσίας τῶν δαιμονίων· πιστεύομεν οὖν (ἐν) τῇ ἀληθείᾳ (εἰς τὴν ἀλήθειαν) τοῦ εὐαγγελίου. 5. οὐ θεραπεύει ἡ παρθένος τὰς νόσους, ὦ προφῆτα, ἀλλὰ φιλεῖ τὰ τέκνα καὶ τηρεῖ τὰς ἐντολὰς τοῦ Θεοῦ. 6. κηρύσσει ὁ υἱὸς τοῦ ἀνθρώπου ἐκ τοῦ πλοίου τοῖς μαθηταῖς καὶ ἀκούουσι(ν) καὶ γράφουσι(ν) τοὺς λόγους τοῖς τέκνοις τοῦ οἰκοδεσπότου.

CHAPTER 6

1. My children therefore are walking with the holy (saintly) young men from the lake (sea) to (towards) the first village; for the unjust (unrighteous) householder is calling. 2. Men do not see the kingdom of heaven in the world, but in our hearts we believe (trust) in the Son. 3. In the last days the holy apostles preach my gospel to the faithful disciples. 4. Brother, the righteous words of your good son save our evil (wicked) children from death; for they bear witness to the truth of the first prophets. 5. You have not money (no money) in your houses, but you save the last loaves for the faithful slaves. 6. You (sing.) speak good words in love.

1. μαρτυροῦσι(ν) (μαρτυρεῖ)* ἡ εἰρήνη καὶ ἡ ἀγάπη τῇ ἀληθείᾳ τοῦ εὐαγγελίου. 2. ἐν τῇ ἡμετέρᾳ κώμῃ τηροῦσι(ν) οἱ δίκαιοι ἀδελφοὶ τὰς ἁγίας ἐντολὰς τοῦ Θεοῦ· ἐν δὲ τῇ ὑμετέρᾳ ἐκκλησίᾳ οὐχ εὑρίσκουσι(ν) οἱ μαθηταὶ τὴν ἀλήθειαν. 3. φιλεῖ ὁ πρῶτος νεανίας τὰ παιδία καὶ λαλεῖ ταῖς πισταῖς παρθένοις ἐν τῷ ἐσχάτῳ οἴκῳ τῆς ἐμῆς κώμης. 4. κρύπτεις τὴν σὴν δικαιοσύνην, λαλεῖ (λαλοῦσι(ν)) δὲ τὰ σὰ ἔργα πρὸ τοῦ Κυρίου. 5. πῶς πείθει ἡ πονηρὰ γλῶσσα τῶν δαιμονίων καὶ τοὺς ἡμετέρους ἀγαθοὺς καὶ ἁγίους δούλους;

* When there are two or more subjects, a preceding verb is often found in the singular to agree with the singular noun immediately following.

CHAPTER 7

1. Jesus therefore was walking with the disciples towards the lake (sea) and many were following. 2. In the big village I used to find many little children and lead them away through the roads to our house; for I love good children. 3. How were the faithful slaves throwing (i.e. casting) (used the faithful slaves to cast) the nets out of the boat into the great lake (sea)? 4. You were asking (used to ask) for holy bread from the temple, not from heaven. 5. From the tongue of Jesus the brothers used to hear the words of eternal life. 6. Because of (on account of) your righteousness you used to read (were reading) the first book of the law, but did not know the gospel.* 7. We therefore were following (used to follow) Jesus even into the desert. 8. Jesus used to cast out demons (devils), but comfort little children.

1. διὰ (τὴν) νόσον ἀπέθνησκον πολλοὶ μαθηταὶ ἐν τῇ ἐρήμῳ, θεραπεύει δὲ ὁ δίκαιος ἀπόστολος τοὺς πιστοὺς (ἀνθρώπους). 2. ὠνομάζομεν (τὸν) Ἰησοῦν τὸν υἱὸν τοῦ ἀνθρώπου καὶ ἐγράφομεν τὰς ἐντολὰς τοῦ ἁγίου εὐαγγελίου ἐν τοῖς ἡμετέροις βιβλίοις. 3. πέμπει ὁ πονηρὸς οἰκοδεσπότης πολλὰ τέκνα εἰς τὴν ἔρημον· ἀποθνήσκουσι(ν)† οὖν. 4. ἀπέκτεινεν ὁ ὑμέτερος ἄδικος δεσπότης (κύριος) πολλοὺς τῶν ἐμῶν πιστῶν δούλων· οὐ γὰρ ἐγίνωσκε τοὺς λόγους τοῦ νόμου. 5. (ὦ) νεανία, ἐζήτεις τὴν βασιλείαν τοῦ οὐρανοῦ· βλέπεις οὖν διὰ τὰ σὰ ἀγαθὰ ἔργα τὰ σημεῖα τοῦ Θεοῦ καὶ πείθει (πείθουσι(ν)) τὴν σὴν καρδίαν.

CHAPTER 8

NB The alternative translations of the genitive (e.g. God's word, the word of God), the constructions possible with πιστεύω (dative

---

* It would be cumbersome here, and often elsewhere, to translate as you used not, when the continuity of the imperfect is implicit in the context.

† Such a construction according to sense is common practice. The subject is still, strictly speaking, the neuter plural τέκνα, but the verb is plural because they are persons.

or preposition) and the optional ν at the end of the 3rd pl. present
indic. active should now be familiar and in future only one will be
used. If the student has used the alternative he may assume its
correctness.

1. The Pharisees do not love (like) these wealthy Romans; for
because (on account) of (their) sins they are not holy. 2. Then in
those days you (sing.) used to teach the crowd; but now you are
blind, for the apostle does not heal this disease. 3. These your
children (children of yours) were throwing (used to throw) my
clothes out of that first boat into the lake (sea); for they are many
(numerous) and wicked. 4. The works of this girl are good, but
the (her) heart is not faithful. 5. O blessed prophets, you used to
bear witness to the truth; but the baptist preaches to the poor in
the desert, for the last of the prophets is righteous and holy.

1. ἐν (δὲ) ταῖς ἡμέραις τῶν προφητῶν ᾠκοδόμουν (οἱ) πλούσιοι
(ἄνθρωποι) πολλοὺς οἴκους ἐν ταύτῃ τῇ κώμῃ. 2. ἐδιδάσκομεν
τοὺς υἱοὺς τούτων τῶν καλῶν παρθένων σὺν τοῖς παιδίοις ἐκείνοις.
3. ἠσθίετε τοῦτον τὸν καλὸν (ἀγαθὸν) ἄρτον καὶ ἐπέμπετε ἄρτους
τοῖς πιστοῖς δούλοις. 4. ἦς (ἦσθα) ἐν τῷ πλοίῳ τούτῳ καὶ
ἀνεγίνωσκες τούτοις τοῖς παιδίοις τὰς ἐσχάτας ἐντολὰς ἐκείνου τοῦ
ἀγαθοῦ (καλοῦ) νόμου. 5. διὰ ταῦτα τὰ πονηρὰ ἔργα ἀπέκτεινον
οἱ Ῥωμαῖοι (τοὺς) δούλους ἐν τῷ σταυρῷ. 6. ἐζήτει ὁ πλούσιος
(ἄνθρωπος) οὗτος μέγαν οἶκον τῷ μακαρίῳ υἱῷ τοῦ οἰκοδεσπότου.

CHAPTER 9

ἄξω, γράψω, βλέψω, ἠγόρασε(ν), ἀπεκάλυψε(ν), ἐβάστασε(ν),
ἐδίωξε(ν), ἐξέκοψε(ν), ἡτοίμασε(ν), ἔκραξε(ν), ἔπραξε(ν), ἐφύ-
λαξε(ν), ἤκουσαν, ᾔτησαν, παρεκάλεσαν, ἐθεράπευσαν.

NB Be careful to distinguish between ὅτι *because* (conjunction
with verb) and διὰ *because of*, with accusative of noun.

1. The Jews therefore sent these wicked robbers (bandits) to the
Romans, for they had no authority. 2. We will write these holy

words in the book and will not reveal (them) to the unrighteous multitude. 3. Then Jesus carried the cross, but the disciples did not follow. 4. O rich young man, you bought clothes for the poor, but you guard much money in the temple. 5. Those slaves will pursue the wicked messenger into this land, for they are good and faithful. 6. Because he cried out in the desert the crowds heard (listened to) the baptist and did (performed) the commandments of the law. 7. How did you (sing.) cut down those big trees?

1. ἠγόρασαν οἱ Ἰουδαῖοι σταυρὸν τῷ υἱῷ τοῦ ἀνθρώπου καὶ ἐτέλεσας τὸ σὸν ἔργον, ὦ Ἰησοῦ. 2. διὰ ταύτην τὴν ἁμαρτίαν τοῦ κόσμου ἔπεμψεν ὁ Θεὸς τὸν Ἰησοῦν εἰς (πρὸς) τὴν γῆν καὶ ἔσωσε τοὺς ἀνθρώπους. 3. ἑτοιμάσετε ὁδὸν τῷ Κυρίῳ ἐν τῇ ἐρήμῳ· φυλάσσει γὰρ καὶ σώσει τοὺς πιστοὺς καὶ ἁγίους (pl. necessary for collective group). 4. ἐν ταύτῃ τῇ ἡμέρᾳ ἐκήρυξαν δέκα ἀπόστολοι τὸ εὐαγγέλιον πολλοῖς ἐν ἐκείνῳ τῷ μεγάλῳ ὄχλῳ. 5. ᾔτησα βιβλίον καὶ ἔγραψα ταῦτα τοῖς ἐμοῖς τέκνοις, ὅτι πιστεύουσιν ἐν τῷ Θεῷ καὶ μαρτυρήσουσι τοῖς σημείοις τοῦ Ἰησοῦ. 6. ἐκρύψαμεν τὸν τυφλὸν (ἄνθρωπον) ἐν τῷ οἴκῳ τούτῳ· ἀπέκτεινον γὰρ οἱ λῃσταὶ τοὺς πλουσίους καὶ ἐλάμβανον τὸ ἀργύριον τῶν πτωχῶν. 7. πῶς ἀπεκάλυψεν ὁ πρῶτος ἀπόστολος τὸ εὐαγγέλιον;

CHAPTER 10

1. I loosed their chains and sent some to the sea (lake), others into this village. 2. Your slaves and our children were reading (used to read) the same books, for they love the words of the holy apostle. 3. The rich and unjust (unrighteous) tax-collector himself used to take his clothes from the poor man; for he (the latter, cf. Latin *hic*) had no money. 4. (But) after these days even sinners (sinners also) will see the kingdom of heaven, for Jesus will persuade them. 5. You, (O) master, said these things against this prophet because you are hostile and persecute us. 6. According to your law we sent that sinner with the same slaves to the Roman himself; but he did not keep them in his own house. 7. When did you (sing.) see the Lord?

9

1. οἱ μὲν ἔπινον οἶνον μετὰ τῶν τελωνῶν (σὺν τοῖς τελώναις), ὁ δὲ ἤσθιον ἄρτον μεθ᾽ ὑμῶν (σὺν ὑμῖν) ἐν τῇ αὐτῇ κώμῃ. 2. ζητοῦσι οἱ ἐχθροί μου (οἱ ἐμοὶ ἐχ.) τὴν γῆν ἡμῶν (τὴν ἡμετέραν γῆν) καὶ συνάξουσιν τὰ πρόβατα ἡμῶν (τὰ ἡμέτερα πρ.) καὶ διώξουσιν ἡμᾶς εἰς τὴν ἔρημον. 3. (ὑμεῖς) αὐτοὶ ἐφυλάξατε τὸν ἀγαθὸν (καλὸν) ἰατρόν, ὅτι ἐθεράπευσε τοὺς τυφλοὺς υἱοὺς ὑμῶν (τοὺς ὑμετέρους τ. υ.)· οἱ δὲ ἐμαρτύρησαν κατ᾽ αὐτοῦ. 4. ὁ (δὲ) δίκαιος οἰκοδεσπότης οὐκ ἐπίστευσεν ἑαυτῷ ἀλλὰ ταῖς ἐντολαῖς τοῦ Θεοῦ· ἀπεκάλυψε γὰρ τὸ εὐαγγέλιον τοῦ Ἰησοῦ αὐτὰς αὐτῷ. 5. διὰ τοῦτο, ὦ νεανία, ἔγραψας ταῦτα (τὰ αὐτὰ) ἐν τῷ βιβλίῳ τοῦ τελώνου κατὰ τοῦ ἀδελφοῦ ἡμῶν (τοῦ ἡμετέρου ἀδ.)· ὁ δὲ (ἀλλ᾽) οὐ πιστεύσει σοι καὶ λαλήσει μοι τὴν ἀλήθειαν. 6. καλὴ ἦν αὕτη ἡ πτωχὴ παρθένος· πολλοὶ οὖν ἐζήτουν αὐτήν, αὐτὴ δ᾽ ἐφίλει τὸν τυφλὸν υἱὸν τοῦ πλουσίου, ὅτι εἶχε μέγαν οἶκον καὶ πολὺ ἀργύριον.

CHAPTER 11

1. Against me. He sends you (sing.) his own children. You (pl.) love yourselves. They were seeking (used to seek) (for) us. We proclaimed (preached) to you (pl.). 2. One prayed to God, the other cried out in the desert. 3. How do (the) tax-collectors and sinners enter the kingdom of heaven before us (the) Pharisees? 4. Jesus chose his apostles from the people and they followed him. 5. Therefore we receive into the holy church both the lame and the poor according to the commandment of our Lord himself. 6. (But or and) in the last days Jesus himself will come and will summon the dead and save them from the authority of the devil. 7. You (sing.) used to receive the unrighteous into your house and prepare bread and wine for them; because (on account) of this therefore many used to come to you and love (you). 8. The slave-girl used to wash (was washing) the child, but he himself used to wash (was washing) his (own) head. 9. Therefore he will be great and will save the people.

1. οἱ μὲν θεραπεύουσιν, οἱ δὲ κηρύσσουσιν. ὁ υἱὸς αὐτοῦ. τὰ παιδία ἡμῶν (τὰ ἡμέτερα π.). ἀκολουθήσομέν σοι. οὐ μαρτυρῶ

ἐμαυτῷ. 2. σύ, ὦ Κύριε, ἐξελέξω τοῦτον (τὸν ἄνθρωπον)· πολλοὺς δὲ (καὶ π.) ἄξει καὶ ἀποκαλύψει αὐτοῖς τὸ εὐαγγέλιόν σου (τὸ σὸν εὐ.) ἐν τοῖς βιβλίοις ἑαυτοῦ (αὐτοῦ). 3. οἱ (μὲν) πονηροὶ (ἄνθρωποι) προσεύχονται τῷ διαβόλῳ αὐτῷ, ὁ δὲ Ἰησοῦς ἐκβάλλει (τὰ) δαιμόνια διὰ τὴν ἐξουσίαν ἑαυτοῦ (αὐτοῦ). 4. ἐδιδάσκετε πολλοὺς τυφλοὺς (ἀνθρώπους) μετὰ τούτων τῶν δέκα παρθένων (σὺν ταύταις ταῖς δ. παρθένοις)· αἱ δὲ ἀνεγίνωσκον αὐτοῖς τοὺς λόγους τῆς αἰωνίου ζωῆς. 5. ἐποιησάμην τὸ πρῶτον βιβλίον, ὦ Θεόφιλε, ὅτι οἱ ἀδελφοί μου (οἱ ἐμοὶ ἀδ.) οὐ προσηύχοντο ἐν ταῖς καρδίαις αὐτῶν (ἑαυτῶν), ἀλλ᾽ ἔλεγον (ἐλάλουν) πονηρὰ κατὰ τῆς ἐκκλησίας. 6. ἐκεῖνος ὁ χωλὸς (ἄνθρωπος) δέξεται τὸν ἄρτον ὅτι αἰτεῖ (αἰτεῖται) κατὰ (τὸν) νόμον.

CHAPTER 12

ἠλέησε(ν), ἀπεκάλυψε(ν), εἶχες, εἶχου, ζητούμεθα, σωζόμεθα, δέξονται, πορεύσονται, ἔρχεται, ἐλεύσεται, ἠτήσασθε, περιεβλέψασθε.

NB From now on only one of the alternative translations will be given for the imperfect, possessive adjectives, θάλασσα, διά with acc.

1. The poor used to be killed with (by) (the) sword by the wicked tax-collectors, while they were journeying through the desert into this land. 2. The synagogue is being built with big stones by the same workmen and after many days they will finish the work, but not on the sabbath. 3. Because he pitied the multitude Jesus summoned them (called them to him), but they were not persuaded by his words. 4. Until I received baptism (was baptized) in the river Jordan I used not to pray to God in repentance, for I used to be led into sin by the devil and his demons. 5. The nets are thrown (cast) by Peter from the boat into the lake. 6. Many were baptized and are walking in the way of righteousness.

11

1. βαστάζεται ὁ μέγας σταυρὸς ὑπὸ τοῦ Ἰησοῦ, ἀλλ᾽ οὐκ ἐλεεῖται ὑπὸ τοῦ ὄχλου. 2. περιεβλεψάμεθα τὸ ἱερὸν καὶ ἐλαλήσαμεν τοῖς παιδίοις· ἠλεήσαμεν γὰρ αὐτούς. 3. ἕως (ὡς, ἐν ᾧ) ἐγράφετο τὸ ἔσχατον εὐαγγέλιον ἐκρύπτοντο ὑπὸ τοὺς λίθους αἱ γραφαὶ ὑπὸ τοῦ πιστοῦ ἀποστόλου τούτου. 4. ἐδέξω τὸν μισθὸν τῆς σῆς δικαιοσύνης ὅτε (ὡς) ἔβλεψας τὸν Ἰησοῦν τοῖς ἰδίοις ὀφθαλμοῖς (σου)· ἐν δὲ ταῖς ἐσχάταις ἡμέραις ἐλεύσεται ἐν τῇ δόξῃ αὐτοῦ μετὰ τῶν ἁγίων ἀγγέλων (σὺν τοῖς ἁγίοις ἀγγέλοις). 5. ἐδιώκεσθε εἰς τὴν ἔρημον ὑπὸ πολλῶν λῃστῶν ἕως (μέχρι, ἄχρι) ὁ κύριος (δεσπότης) ἡμῶν ἔπεμψε τοὺς δούλους αὐτοῦ. 6. οὐκ ἀνεγινώσκοντο αἱ γραφαὶ αὗται ὑπὸ τῶν νεανιῶν· ἐφυλάσσοντο γὰρ ὑπὸ τοῦ ἀδίκου τελώνου ἐν τῷ ἰδίῳ οἴκῳ (αὐτοῦ).

CHAPTER 13

1. This blind man whose eyes Jesus healed did not sin. 2. The Galileans will flee into Samaria, but the enemy will find them there. 3. The disciples learnt these things in Rome in which (where) Paul left them. 4. And it came to pass, after a long time the girl bore a son, who led many to salvation. 5. We did not drink wine until we (had) looked round the temple. 6. My little children fell out of the boat and five died in the sea (were drowned); because of this their bad teacher suffered many things (i.e. greatly). 7. While he was saying this a great sign (miracle) happened (came) from heaven (the sky).

1. πέντε (μὲν) ἔλαβον τὸν μισθὸν ἑαυτῶν καὶ ἀπελεύσονται ἐν εἰρήνῃ, ὁ δὲ ἐργάτης οὗτος ἔχει νόσον ἣν θεραπεύσει ὁ ἰατρὸς ὧδε. 2. ἠγάγομεν τὰ ἡμέτερα πρόβατα πρὸς τὸν μέγαν ποταμὸν εἰς ὃν ἔπεσεν (ἔπεσον)· ἐκεῖ δ᾽ ἐλίπομεν αὐτά. 3. λήμψεσθε (δέξεσθε) σωτηρίαν ἐκ τῶν ἐχθρῶν ὑμῶν, οἳ ἥμαρτον ὅτε (ὡς) ἐλάλησαν κατὰ τοῦ Θεοῦ. 4. μέγας γενήσεται καὶ ὁ λαὸς τῶν Ἰουδαίων καλέσει αὐτὸν Ἰωάννην τὸν βαπτιστήν, ὅτι βαπτίσει πολλοὺς ἐν τῷ Ἰορδάνῃ ποταμῷ. 5. εὖρες ὧδε τὸ ἀργύριον ὃ ἔλιπεν ὁ ἀδελφός μου ὑπὸ τὸν μέγαν λίθον ἐκεῖνον ὃς φυλάσσεται (ἐν) ταῖς μαχαίραις τῶν δούλων.

CHAPTER 14

ἔμαθες, ἔτεκες, ἐφύγομεν, ἀπεθάνομεν, ἐλάβετο, ἐγένετο, εὑρήσονται,
πίονται, ἔγραψας, ἐγράψω, ᾔτησας, ᾔτήσω, ἠγόρασας, ἠγοράσω.

1. Simon therefore bore Christ's cross until they came to the place
in which (where) he died. 2. The attendants said that they had
not found (did not find) the apostles in the prison in which they left
them. 3. And it came to pass, when we went out from Nazareth
he saw a widow and said that he pitied her. 4. And when they
ate (had eaten) the five loaves they departed to their own homes.
5. And immediately they came to the land of the Gerasenes.
There when they went out of the boat (disembarked) they saw a
man who was tormented by many demons which were called
Legion. 6. You Pharisees told us that you knew the commandments of the law; but this Stephen bore witness to the truth and
walks in the way of eternal life, for he is a faithful and good
minister of the church.

1. ὅτε (ὡς) ἠκούσαμεν τὴν φωνὴν τοῦ κυρίου (δεσπότου) ἡμῶν
εὐθὺς εἴπομεν ὅτι προσεύχεται. 2. ἕτερος (δὲ) στρατιώτης εἶπεν
ὅτι ἔκραξεν ὁ Ἰησοῦς μεγάλη φωνῇ. 3. διήλθετε τὴν γῆν (διὰ τῆς
γῆς) ἡμῶν καὶ ἐμάθετε ὅτι ἀποθνήσκει (ἀποθνήσκουσι) πολλὰ τέκνα
ἐν τοῖς ἀγροῖς. 4. πολλοὶ (δ᾽) ἐφοβοῦντο τὸν διάβολον, ἕως (μέχρι,
ἄχρι) εἶδον (ἔβλεψαν less common) τὸν Ἰησοῦν καὶ ἔσωσεν αὐτούς.
5. ὅτι ἠλέησα τοῦτον τὸν χωλὸν (ἄνθρωπον) εἶπον ὅτι ἐλεύσομαι
(πορεύσομαι) μετ᾽ αὐτοῦ (σὺν αὐτῷ) καὶ ἄξω (αὐτὸν) πρὸς τὸν
ἰατρόν. 6. εἶπεν ὁ πιστὸς δοῦλος ὅτι διῆλθε τὴν ἔρημον (διὰ τῆς
ἐρήμου) ὁ κύριος (δεσπότης) αὐτοῦ καὶ ἔλιπεν ἐκεῖ τὰ πρόβατα
αὐτοῦ.

CHAPTER 15

1. Mary rejoiced when the angel greeted her, for he said to her
that she would bear a son who would be called Jesus because he
would save his people. The girl (maiden) therefore said to him

that she was the handmaid of the Lord. 2. Jesus therefore went down into the desert and there he fasted forty days. Later when he was tempted by the devil he said to him that it was written, Thou shalt not tempt the Lord thy God. 3. As it was said in the parable, these were sown on the good ground and bear much fruit. 4. After the death of Jesus we were with him until he was taken up from us into heaven. 5. The ten lepers rejoiced when they were cleansed by Jesus. 6. You knew in your own hearts that your words would not be heard, but you prayed to God and he saved you. 7. When did you remember the word which was spoken by the wise young man?

1. μακάριοί (εἰσιν) οἱ πτωχοί· ὕστερον γὰρ ἔσονται πλούσιοι.
2. διωχθήσεσθε ὑπὸ τῶν Ἰουδαίων ὅτι ἔγνωτέ με καὶ τὰ ἔργα μου.
3. κρυβήσεται αὕτη ἡ γραφὴ ἀπὸ τῶν σοφῶν, ἀλλ᾽ ἀποκαλυφθήσεται (τοῖς) παιδίοις. 4. ἠγοράσθησαν πέντε ἄρτοι, ἀλλ᾽ οὐκ ἐσώθησαν ἀπὸ τῶν ἐχθρῶν, οἳ εὐθὺς ἔφαγον αὐτούς. 5. ὁ (δὲ) Ἰησοῦς ἐπορεύθη μετὰ τῶν μαθητῶν (σὺν τοῖς μαθηταῖς) αὐτοῦ πρὸς τὴν θάλασσαν· ἐκεῖ δ᾽ εὗρον μέγαν ὄχλον τῶν Ἰουδαίων, ὧν οἱ μὲν ἐπείσθησαν ὑπ᾽ αὐτοῦ, οἱ δὲ οὐκ ἤχθησαν εἰς μετάνοιαν. 6. ἐρρέθη (ἐρρήθη) ὑπὸ τοῦ προφήτου ὅτι ὄψονται (βλέψουσιν) οἱ ἁμαρτωλοὶ τὴν σωτηρίαν τοῦ Θεοῦ καὶ χαρήσονται.

CHAPTER 16

1. Jesus went up to Jerusalem, for he knew that there he was about to suffer much (greatly). He therefore exhorted his disciples to carry their own crosses and follow him. 2. And it came to pass, when Jesus finished these words he departed into the fields (countryside) to teach others. 3. The disciples therefore began to go out to the uttermost parts (ends) of the earth; for Jesus commanded them to proclaim to men that the kingdom of heaven was approaching. 4. When Jesus was about to die he cried out with a loud voice. 5. We begged the attendant not to receive (accept) the money. He was unwilling (refused) to hear (listen), but rejoiced when he received the reward of his iniquity (wrongdoing). 6. You

(sing.) were unwilling to journey (go) with us through the fields. Because of this therefore we now command you not to go with us to see these signs (miracles).

1. ἐκέλευσεν ὁ προφήτης τὸν λαὸν (προσέταξε τῷ λαῷ) ἑτοιμάσαι ὁδὸν τῷ Κυρίῳ. 2. οὐκ ἠθελήσαμεν (ἠθέλομεν, ἐβουλήθημεν, ἐβουλόμεθα) γράφειν ταῦτα (τὰ αὐτὰ) ὑμῖν. 3. ᾔτησάς με ἐλεεῖν (ἐλεῆσαι) τοῦτον τὸν πτωχὸν καὶ πέμψαι αὐτὸν πρὸς τὸν ἐμὸν οἶκον. 4. ἤρξατο ὁ Ἰησοῦς πολλὰ διδάσκειν τὸν λαόν. 5. δέομαί σου τηρεῖν τοῦτον τὸν οἶνον, ὅτι ὁ κύριός (δεσπότης) μου ἐκέλευσε τὰς παρθένους (διέταξε, διετάξατο ταῖς παρθένοις) μὴ πιεῖν (πίνειν). 6. ἤλθετε μετὰ τοῦ ἀδελφοῦ (σὺν τῷ ἀδελφῷ, συνήλθετε τῷ ἀδ.) ὑμῶν διδάσκεσθαι ἐν τούτῳ τῷ τόπῳ. 7. ἐπείσθησαν οἱ ἁμαρτωλοὶ οὗτοι (ἐν) τοῖς σοφοῖς λόγοις αὐτοῦ φοβεῖσθαι τὸν Κύριον ἐν ταῖς καρδίαις ἑαυτῶν καὶ ποιεῖν (πράσσειν) δίκαια ἔργα.

CHAPTER 17

ἄξειν, ἄξεσθαι, ἀχθήσεσθαι, σώσειν, σώσεσθαι, σωθήσεσθαι, πέμψειν, πέμψεσθαι, πεμφθήσεσθαι, ζητεῖν, ζητεῖσθαι, πειράζειν, πειράζεσθαι, μαθεῖν, κρύψαι, αἰτήσασθαι, προσεύξασθαι, κηρυχθῆναι, κληθῆναι.

1. While Jesus and his disciples were journeying to Jerusalem he said that the son of man must suffer many things (much, greatly). 2. It is not lawful (permissible) for us to know well (rightly) the time at which (the) Christ will come, but because he said these things we learnt that on that day the saints would see him. 3. After John heard in prison (of) the works of Christ he sent disciples to talk (speak) to him; but he ordered them to say to (tell) their teacher what they heard and saw. 4. Well therefore did he say that the righteous had no need of repentance because they were not sinners. 5. The Pharisees used to pray wrongly in the roads (streets) in order to be heard by men and to receive (obtain) glory. 6. In the last days the sun will be hidden, but the saints will rejoice because of Christ's coming (because Christ has

15

come) back (again) to earth.   7. He said therefore that before
reading (he read) the old scriptures he did not believe the words of
the teacher who ordered the rich to help the poor justly (righteously).   8. This girl is ill, but the wise doctor will heal the
disease.   9. How will the Lord save the world?

1. διὰ τὸ εὐαγγελίσασθαι τοὺς ἀποστόλους ἐν τούτῳ τῷ τόπῳ, ὦ
ἀδελφοί μου, μεγάλη ἔσται ἡ χαρὰ ὑμῶν.   2. ἤνεγκον οὗτοι οἱ
νεανίαι κράββατον εἰς (πρὸς) τὸ ἰδεῖν τὸν Ἰησοῦν τὸν χωλὸν καὶ
θεραπεῦσαι αὐτόν.   3. δικαίως ἐμαρτύρησαν οἱ κριταὶ τῷ παλαιῷ
νόμῳ ἐν τῷ φυλάσσειν αὐτοὺς τὸν λαόν.   4. μετὰ τὸ πάλιν ἐλθεῖν
τὸν Ἰησοῦν πρὸς τὴν θάλασσαν ἐκέλευσε τὸν μαθητὴν (ἐπέταξε τῷ
μαθητῇ) βαλεῖν τὸ δίκτυον αὐτοῦ ἐκ τοῦ πλοίου.   5. δεῖ ἀγαθὸν
κριτὴν εὖ τηρεῖν τὰς ἐντολὰς διὰ τὸ γραφῆναι αὐτὰς ὑπὸ τοῦ Θεοῦ
διὰ τοῦ μεγάλου προφήτου.   6. οὐκ ἠθέλομεν πορευθῆναι διὰ τῆς
γῆς ταύτης εἰς (πρὸς) τὸ μανθάνειν (μαθεῖν) ἀπὸ τοῦ σοφοῦ
στρατιώτου.

CHAPTER 18

1. Immediately therefore four guards journeyed to their native
place to see this great sign (miracle).   2. After the cock crows
(cock-crow) we shall come back (again) to the ruler's vineyard
because we wish to drink the good wine with the shepherds.
3. You die in hope because you trust (believe) that the soul will
have life for ever.   4. How will (shall) flesh and blood see the
kingdom of heaven which is about to come (going to come) in
those days?   5. The saviour was sent into the world to preach
(proclaim) the word to governors and rulers and the poor.   6. In
the name of Christ they will do great works in order to persuade
men that his mouth used to speak faithful (trustworthy) and
righteous (just) sayings.   7. Again he cried out that through the
body we found the reward (wages) of death, but that through the
Holy Spirit we were saved from the authority of the devil.   8. Where
did you find this beautiful (fine) cock?

1. ἔγνω ὅτι δεῖ τὸν πλούσιον ἄρχοντα ὠφελεῖν τοὺς πτωχοὺς κριτάς.
2. ἤνεγκον οἱ πονηροὶ φύλακες πολὺν καρπὸν τῷ ἀδίκῳ ἡγεμόνι ἀπὸ (ἐκ) τοῦ ἀμπελῶνος τοῦ ἄρχοντος. 3. σοφῶς ἤγαγον οἱ δέκα ἀγαθοὶ ποιμένες τὰ πρόβατα αὐτῶν ἀπὸ (ἐκ) τῆς ἐρήμου εἰς τὴν (ἰδίαν) πατρίδα ἑαυτῶν. 4. διὰ τοῦ ἁγίου πνεύματος ἐξῆλθεν (ἐξῆλθον) ἀγαθὰ (καλὰ) ῥήματα ἐκ τοῦ στόματος τοῦ σωτῆρος. 5. ἐν τῷ αἰῶνι τούτῳ διωχθήσεσθε ὑπὸ τῶν πονηρῶν, ὕστερον δὲ λήμψεσθε (δέξεσθε) τὸν μισθὸν ὑμῶν καὶ γενήσεσθε μεγάλοι ἐν τῷ οὐρανῷ. 6. τότε εἶπεν ὁ Ἰησοῦς ὅτι δεῖ ἡμᾶς φαγεῖν τὴν σάρκα αὐτοῦ καὶ πιεῖν τὸ αἷμα.

CHAPTER 19

1. Your Father (who is) in heaven numbers even the hairs of your heads. 2. After Jesus had been baptized in the river when he came up from the water a voice was heard out of the clouds. 3. Men have ears in order to hear (for hearing) and feet to walk (for walking). 4. The father fell at Jesus' knees and begged him to help his son. He immediately healed him. 5. (O) woman, I tell you that you had five husbands and now he (the one) whom you have is not your husband. 6. Some bought oil for the (their) lamps, but others had none and marvelled at the wisdom of the wise virgins. 7. (O) Father, you will pity us, for tax-collectors and sinners are sanctified by your grace. 8. Women ought not to (must not) uncover their hair in church.

1. διὰ τὴν χάριν τοῦ Θεοῦ ἐγένετο ἀπόστολος μετὰ τὸ ἀκοῦσαι αὐτὸν τὴν φωνὴν τοῦ Κυρίου τοῖς ἰδίοις ὡσί(ν). 2. ἤθελεν (ἠθέλησεν, ἐβούλετο, ἐβουλήθη) ὁ ἀγαθὸς ἡγεμὼν πέμψαι τὴν μητέρα καὶ τὴν θυγατέρα μου πρὸς (εἰς) τὴν ἰδίαν πατρίδα ἑαυτῶν εἰς (πρὸς) τὸ σώζεσθαι αὐτὰς ἀπὸ (ἐκ) τῶν ἐχθρῶν. 3. νὺξ ἦν καὶ ἤρξατο ὁ Ἰησοῦς περιπατεῖν (περιπατῆσαι) ἐπὶ τοῦ ὕδατος (τὸ ὕδωρ, τῷ ὕδατι) ἀπὸ τῆς γῆς πρὸς τὸ πλοῖον· οἱ δὲ μαθηταὶ εἶδον αὐτὸν τοῖς ἰδίοις ὀφθαλμοῖς καὶ ἐφοβήθησαν (ἐφοβοῦντο). 4. ἐβάστασας τὸν καρπὸν ἐκ (ἀπὸ) τοῦ ἀμπελῶνος ἐν ταῖς σαῖς χερσὶ καὶ ἔλιπες αὐτὸν ἐπὶ τῇ θύρᾳ τοῦ οἴκου τοῦ ποιμένος. 5. ἔφαγον οἱ κύνες τὴν σάρκα

τοῦ νεκροῦ τοῖς ὀδοῦσιν αὐτῶν. 6. δεῖ τοὺς ἄνδρας καὶ τὰς γυναῖκας πείθειν τὰ τέκνα ἑαυτῶν περιπατεῖν (πορεύεσθαι) δικαίως ἐν τῇ ὁδῷ τοῦ Κυρίου.

CHAPTER 20

γλώσσης, μαθητοῦ, φύλακος, πρόβατον, λαμπάδα, σωτῆρα, χεῖρας, τρίχας, γόνατα, ποσί(ν), κυσί(ν), αἰῶσι(ν), ἄρχουσι(ν), ἦρξε(ν), ἦρξατο, ἤρχθη, ἔπεμψε(ν), ἐπέμψατο, ἐπέμφθη, ἠγόρασε(ν), ἠγοράσατο, ἠγοράσθη, ᾔτησε(ν), ᾐτήσατο, ᾐτήθη.

1. Through the hands of the apostles God did many mighty works, for they healed with oil many who had diseases and released (them) from their tribulations. 2. After the resurrection of the dead there will be judgment on (the) earth and you (the) twelve apostles will have thrones and will be judges of the nations (Gentiles). 3. The heart of the multitude (whole body) was faithful and they did not fear (were not afraid of) the king and his guards and attendants. 4. John had (used to have) a girdle (belt) round his loins (hips) and a cloak which was made from camel's hair. 5. O king, the high priest will come and will exhort (urge) you to send Jesus back to the governor. 6. The saviour went away (departed) to the mountain and there he taught the crowds until night fell (literally: happened; it was night). 7. This child took a big fish out of the water which the lord (owner) of the vineyard bought. 8. These (men) died in hope, for they knew that the ruler of this world was not going to (would not) have power and authority for ever.

1. ἐν τούτῳ τῷ ἔτει διὰ τὴν χάριν τοῦ Θεοῦ ἐλύθην ἀπὸ τῶν δεσμῶν μου ὑπὸ τῶν στρατιωτῶν οἳ ἐφύλασσόν με ἐν τῇ φυλακῇ. 2. μεγάλη ἐγένετο αὕτη ἡ πόλις ἐν τοῖς ἔθνεσιν· πολλοὶ γὰρ ἤγαγον (ἦγον) τοὺς υἱοὺς αὐτῶν εἰς (πρὸς) τὸ ἰδεῖν τὸ ἱερὸν καὶ τὸν καλὸν οἶκον τοῦ βασιλέως. 3. ἐλάλησεν ὁ Ἰησοῦς τοῖς μαθηταῖς περὶ τοῦ ἰδίου τέλους καὶ εἶπεν ὅτι ἔσται ἀνάστασις. 4. (ἐν) (τῇ) πίστει γινώσκομεν ὅτι μετὰ τὸ ἀποθανεῖν τὸν Ἰησοῦν εἶδον πάλιν οἱ

μαθηταὶ αὐτὸν ἐν τῷ σώματι. 5. (ἐν) τοῖς ὀδοῦσιν αὐτῶν ἔσωσαν οἱ κύνες τὸ ἀργύριον ἀπὸ τῶν λῃστῶν οἳ ἐπείρασαν λαβεῖν αὐτό.

CHAPTER 21

1. Those who bless God will receive their own reward. 2. The Jews themselves who received the promises were unwilling to know Christ. 3. He who beholds the son and believes in him will have everlasting life. 4. This seed which was sown on good ground is blessed by God. 5. Those who have repented ought to glorify God because of the forgiveness of (their) sins. 6. This man who became high priest unjustly is wicked. 7. You who drank my cup are about to suffer the same tribulation. 8. Those who dwelt in (the dwellers in, inhabitants of) Jerusalem went out to John in order to be baptized by him. 9. This beloved child who is possessed by demons (a demoniac) used to fall into (the) fire and into (the) water. 10. This is the Christ (Messiah) who will save the world. 11. For the bread of God is he who comes down from heaven. 12. It is necessary for him who follows me to (he who follows me must) carry his cross.

1. μακάριοί (εἰσιν) οἱ ἑτοιμάζοντες ὁδὸν τῷ Κυρίῳ· χαρήσονται γάρ. 2. ἡ (γυνὴ ἡ) βαστάζουσα (φέρουσα) τὴν λαμπάδα θεραπεύει τοὺς πάσχοντας. 3. ἡ μήτηρ μου ἡ τεκοῦσα πέντε υἱοὺς καὶ τέσσαρας θυγατέρας ἔλεγεν ὅτι φιλεῖ ταῦτα τὰ τέκνα ἑαυτῆς. 4. ὁ Πατὴρ ὁ πέμψας (με) ἐκέλευσέ με (προσέταξέ μοι) κηρύσσειν ἄφεσιν (τῶν) ἁμαρτιῶν τοῖς ἀνδράσι καὶ ταῖς γυναιξίν. 5. οἱ ἀπαχθέντες ὑπὸ τῶν φυλάκων ἀπέθανον ἐπὶ τοῦ σταυροῦ (ἐπὶ, ἐν τῷ σταυρῷ). 6. ὁ ἔχων ὦτα ἀκούειν δέξεται (λήμψεται) τὰ ῥήματα ταῦτα.

CHAPTER 22

1. He answered and said that those who reproached God did not bear the fruit of righteousness. 2. Therefore when he had come

down from the mountain he entered the city again (went back into)
to find his daughter there who had a demon (was a demoniac).
3. Therefore if we say that we have no sin we do not speak the
truth about ourselves. 4. When he had opened the door the
robber drove away many sheep. 5. Although she had suffered
much (greatly) in bearing (when she bore) her beloved son the
mother rejoiced when she saw her firstborn little child (baby).
6. When we have confessed (if we confess) our sins we shall
receive forgiveness from the Father. 7. At the tax-collector's
(house) you (sing.) drank much wine and obeyed him when he
ordered you to take the poor widows' money unjustly. 8. Thus
therefore he exhorted the multitude to receive the word, but they
were unwilling to hear (listen), because they did not believe (in)
the gospel. 9. As we were going through the fields we beheld
much fruit and since we had fasted for four days we wished to eat.
10. And because they had done many things contrary to (the) law
they were brought into the city by the guards; but in the presence
of (before) the judge they said that they walked according to (the)
law in the way of the Lord.

1. ὑπάγοντες (ἀπερχόμενοι) ἐθεωρήσαμεν μέγαν (πολὺν) ὄχλον θαυ-
μάζοντα ἐπὶ τῇ πίστει τοῦ τυφλοῦ. 2. καὶ ἀποκριθεὶς εἶπεν ὅτι
ἐξῆλθεν ὁ υἱὸς παρὰ τοῦ Πατρὸς τοῦ πέμψαντος αὐτὸν εἰς τὸν
κόσμον. 3. ὁμολογήσαντες (δὲ) τὰς ἁμαρτίας αὐτῶν περιεπάτησαν
παρὰ τὸν ποταμὸν ἕως (μέχρι, ἄχρι) ἦλθον εἰς τὴν πόλιν. 4. καίπερ
οὕτως πτωχὸς ὢν πειράζω ὠφελεῖν τοὺς μὴ δεχομένους (λαμβά-
νοντας) μισθόν· ἔπεμψα γὰρ ἰχθὺν πρὸς ταύτην τὴν χήραν (ταύτῃ
τῇ χήρᾳ). 5. ἀναβαίνων ἐκ τοῦ ὕδατος εἶδεν ὁ Ἰησοῦς τὸ Ἅγιον
Πνεῦμα καταβαῖνον εἰς (ἐπὶ) αὐτόν. 6. προσευξάμενος (δ’) ἔξω
ἐν ἐρήμοις τόποις εἰσῆλθε πάλιν εἰς τὴν πόλιν πρὸς (εἰς) τὸ εὐαγγελίσασθαι (εὐαγγελίζεσθαι) ἐκεῖ.

CHAPTER 23

1. And when Jesus had been taken up, while the disciples were
gazing into heaven (the sky), a cloud took him from their eyes

(sight). 2. When Paul had chosen elders for our church, the inhabitants of the city were about to kill (on the point of killing) him. 3. When the shepherds saw the star, the young men wanted to leave the sheep on the mountain. 4. My father when he was still a little boy saw Jesus passing by the lake while many followed. 5. As the crowd was (were) no longer listening he immediately ordered the disciples to enter the boat (embark). 6. I shall no longer be with you for a long time (for long), for while the governor is in Rome the centurion who has many soldiers under him is already about to judge me. 7. Therefore you will be persecuted by the Gentiles; for these, as the apostles have not preached the gospel here, are being persuaded that you are doing (acting) wrongly contrary to (the) law. 8. In the time of the prophet Isaiah when that priest had fled from the city, some wished to keep his wife in prison, others not to receive his children into their houses. 9. If you do not bear witness to the faith, many will be walking in darkness, for they will not hear about Jesus, the light of the world. 10. According to his father's wish, though his mother was unwilling, your brother became a bandit (robber). Justly therefore he died upon a cross.

1. ἤδη περιπατοῦντος τοῦ Ἰησοῦ, (ὅτε, ὡς, ἐν ᾧ, ἕως περιεπάτει ὁ Ἰησοῦς, ἐν τῷ περιπατεῖν τὸν Ἰησοῦν) ἐπὶ τοῦ ὕδατος (ἐπὶ τὸ ὕδωρ, ἐπὶ τῷ ὕδατι) ἤρξαντο οἱ μαθηταὶ κράζειν θαυμάζοντες (ὅτι ἐθαύμαζον, διὰ τὸ θαυμάζειν αὐτούς) ἐπὶ τῇ δυνάμει αὐτοῦ. 2. οἱ φύλακες οἱ φυλάσσοντές (οἳ ἐφύλασσόν) με ἐπείσθησαν ὑπὸ τῆς μητρός μου λῦσαί με, (καίπερ) πολλῶν φοβουμένων. 3. ἔτι ἐγγιζουσῶν (προσερχομένων) τῶν γυναικῶν (ὡς, ἐν ᾧ, ἕως ἔτι ἐγγίζουσι αἱ γυναῖκες, ἐν τῷ ἐγγίζειν τὰς γυναῖκας) πρὸς τὴν πόλιν (τῇ πόλει), ἑτοιμάσομεν οἴκους αὐταῖς· θελήσουσι γὰρ κατοικεῖν ὧδε μετὰ τῶν ἀνδρῶν (σὺν τοῖς ἀνδράσιν) αὐτῶν. 4. κηρύξαντος (δὲ) τοῦ Ἰωάννου (ὅτε, ὡς, ἐπεὶ ἐκήρυξεν ὁ Ἰωάννης, μετὰ τὸ κηρύξαι τὸν Ἰωάννην) τῷ ὄχλῳ, πολλοὶ ἐβουλήθησαν (ἠθέλησαν) βαπτισθῆναι. 5. παράγων (δὲ) ὁ Ἰησοῦς (παρῆγε καὶ, ὡς, ἐν ᾧ, ἕως παρῆγε, ἐν τῷ παράγειν τὸν Ἰησοῦν) παρὰ τὴν θάλασσαν εἶδε τὸν Ἰωάννην καὶ τὸν ἀδελφὸν αὐτοῦ βάλλοντας τὰ δίκτυα αὐτῶν ἀπὸ (ἐκ) τοῦ πλοίου εἰς (πρὸς) τὸ λαβεῖν ἰχθύας. 6. θέλοντες (βουλόμενοι, ὅτι ἤθελον, ἐβούλοντο, διὰ τὸ θέλειν, βούλεσθαι) ἰδεῖν

τὸν ἀστέρα τοῖς ἰδίοις ὀφθαλμοῖς ἔλιπον οὗτοι οἱ βασιλεῖς τὴν
πατρίδα ἑαυτῶν· τότε δ' εὗρον τὸ παιδίον παρὰ τῇ μητρὶ μετὰ τῶν
ποιμένων (σὺν τοῖς ποιμέσι) καὶ ἐθαύμασαν.

CHAPTER 24

1. When the cock had roused (wakened) the boy, the mother
ordered him to stay in bed, because it was still early. 2. Who owes
money here to the tax-collector? For he will condemn all those
who do not act according to law. 3. All those therefore who had
been sent forth into the cities to preach the gospel (evangelize)
came back (again, returned) to Capernaum with great joy, when
(or because) many had received the word. 4. Why did you lose
those beautiful (fine) sheep on the mountain today? For the king
himself bought them and sent them forth (despatched) to this field
with their shepherd. 5. A Cyrenean therefore, Simon by name
(named S.), took up Christ's cross and carried it until they came to
the place in which (where) he had to die. 6. I ought to report
(announce) these faithful (trustworthy) sayings to (in) Rome also;
for there I must be judged before (in the presence of) Caesar.
7. Some bandits (robbers) killed my husband with (the) sword, as
he was going through Galilee to his native place. 8. Why do we
not have authority to cast out this demon which (who) is trying to
destroy the boy? 9. When he had been raised from the dead,
after forty days Jesus was taken up into the clouds, while the
disciples gazed into heaven (the sky). 10. When this city had
been destroyed (after the destruction of this city) the enemy wished
to kill the citizens.

1. ὀφείλομεν (δεῖ ἡμᾶς) πέμψαι πάντας τοὺς καρποὺς ἀπὸ τοῦ
ἀμπελῶνος πρὸς τοὺς μένοντας (τοῖς μένουσιν) ἐν τῇ πόλει· νη-
στεύουσι γάρ τινες καὶ ἀποθανοῦνται. 2. ἀποκτείναντες δὲ (μετὰ
τὸ ἀποκτεῖναι) τὸν βασιλέα οἱ πονηροὶ στρατιῶται ἐδεήθησαν τῶν
φυλάκων κρύπτειν αὐτοὺς ἐν τῷ ἱερῷ. 3. οὐ κατακρινοῦμεν τὰς
χήρας τὰς ἀποκτεινάσας (αἳ ἀπέκτειναν) τοὺς ἄνδρας ἑαυτῶν ἀδίκους ὄντας καὶ ποιοῦντας (ὅτι ἄδικοι ἦσαν καὶ ἐποίουν, διὰ τὸ

ἀδίκους αὐτοὺς εἶναι καὶ ποιεῖν) πάντα παρὰ (τὸν) νόμον.   4. τί
ἔφυγον κύνες τινὲς ἀπὸ τοῦ οἴκου ἰδόντες (ὅτε, ὡς, ἐπεὶ εἶδον, ἐν
τῷ ἰδεῖν αὐτοὺς) τὸν παῖδα ἐγγίζοντα (προσερχόμενον) μετὰ τεσ-
σάρων παρθένων (σὺν τέσσαρσι παρθένοις);   5. τίς ἀναγινώσκει
ὅλον τὸ βιβλίον τοῦ προφήτου καὶ ἀναγνοὺς (μετὰ τὸ ἀναγνῶναι)
τηρεῖ ἐν τῇ καρδίᾳ αὐτοῦ πάσας τὰς ἐντολὰς καὶ ἐπαγγελίας;
6. σπείρας (ὅτε, ὡς, ἐπεὶ ἔσπειρε) τὰ σπέρματα ἐπὶ τὴν γῆν (ἐπὶ
τῆς γῆς, ἐπὶ τῇ γῇ) πάλιν ἦλθεν ὁ σπείρων πρὸς (εἰς) τὸν οἶκον
αὐτοῦ εὐλογῶν καὶ δοξάζων τὸν Θεόν.

CHAPTER 25

1. And if your right hand offends (RV) you (causes you to fall
away, Diglot, causes you to sin, RSV, is your undoing NEB), cut it
off and cast it from you (throw it away).   Matt. 5.30.   2. Rise and
walk.   I command you to sin no longer (more).   3. The man who
had the demons (the demoniac) answered and said, Send us into
the swine (hogs).   4. On the third day when he had been raised
(had risen) he went out of (left) the tomb and said to Mary:
'Woman, why are you weeping?'   5. If a strong man has much
money (a lot of money), let him guard it in his own house.   6. Let
all the deaf hear and receive my words in their ears.   7. Let the
body be lifted up on the cross and remain there in order that all
may see this unrighteous (criminal) and wicked robber (bandit)
dying thus.   8. Why did you (sing.) cry out?   For nobody knows
the hour in (at) which the householder (master of the house) is
about (is going) to come.   Therefore I say to you all, 'Pray
(keep on praying)'.   9. When the girl saw the angel and heard what
he said to (told) her she answered and said, 'Let it happen to me
according to your saying'.   10. Lo! I tell you, always ask from
God what you (sing.) wish to receive, for he will pity (have mercy
on) you if you believe that he is good.

1. ἄνοιξον τὸ στόμα σου καὶ ἄγγειλον νῦν (ἤδη) πᾶσι τοῖς ἔθνεσι
τούτοις τὰ σημεῖα καὶ δυνάμεις (μεγάλα ἔργα) τοῦ Κυρίου.   2. εὐλο-
γείτω (εὐλογείτωσαν) τὸν Κύριον ἡ γῆ καὶ πάντες οἱ κατοικοῦντες

(οἳ κατοικοῦσιν) αὐτήν (ἐν αὐτῇ). 3. μένετε παρὰ τῷ μνημείῳ πᾶ-
σαν τὴν νύκτα καὶ φυλάσσετε αὐτό· οὐ δεῖ γὰρ τοὺς κύνας ἐγγίσαι
(προσελθεῖν). 4. πάντοτε φέρετε (βαστάζετε) ἔλαιον ἐν ταῖς λαμ-
πάσιν ὑμῶν. 5. πέμψον (πέμψατε) ἕνα τῶν δύο ἰχθύων τούτων
πρὸς τὸν βασιλέα (τῷ βασιλεῖ)· θέλει (βούλεται) γὰρ φαγεῖν ἰχθὺν
λημφθέντα ἐν ταύτῃ τῇ θαλάσσῃ. 6. τίς κατακρινεῖ τοὺς υἱοὺς
τοῦ Θεοῦ; εὐλογείσθωσαν καὶ δοξαζέσθωσαν καὶ ὑπὸ τῶν ἀγγέλων.

CHAPTER 26

ἀπολοῦμεν, ἀποκτενοῦμεν, ἀροῦμεν, ἀποκρίνασθαι, ἀποκριθῆναι,
αἰτησάτω, αἰτησάσθω, αἰτηθήτω, τηρείτωσαν, τηρείσθωσαν, αἰῶνος,
αἰῶσι(ν), γένους, γένεσι(ν), δυνάμεως, δυνάμεσι(ν), δόξης, δόξαις,
ἰχθύν, χάριν.

1. Greet all the brothers. For these (they) helped me in the
beginning when I had need of bread, when I was dwelling in their
city. 2. He therefore said to the disciples that they were to enter
the boat (told the disciples to embark) and depart. 3. Let us no
longer ask for anything, lest the Gentiles say that we are always
begging. 4. A leper approached and worshipped (made obeisance
to) him and begged (him) to cleanse him (make him clean). 5. And
he touched the tongue of the dumb man and said to him, 'Lo!
you shall talk'. 6. Lady (woman), never shall I see anybody (any
woman) so beautiful. Happy (blessed) is your husband and I
shall command him to treat you well. 7. Do not condemn anyone
before hearing his whole story (all that he has to say). 8. Neither
my father nor my mother sinned. Therefore do not command
that they should be destroyed (them to be destroyed) by (the) wild
beasts. 9. Do not sit on the ground any longer, but stand in the
middle (Mark 3.3, Diglot; stand forth RV; come and stand out
here NEB), for I want to touch you in order that you may walk.
10. Do not fear (stop being afraid), but report (announce) that we
seemed each one (individually) to hear them speaking in our own
language. 11. Jesus said, 'Arise, let us go'. While he was still
speaking, lo! Judas, one of the twelve, came and with him a great

24

crowd with swords from the high priests and elders of the people.
Immediately he approached Jesus and said, 'Hail, Rabbi'.

1. ἄρωμεν τὸν σταυρὸν ἡμῶν καὶ ἀκολουθῶμεν τῷ Ἰησοῦ ἕως
(μέχρι, ἄχρι) τοῦ τέλους, πιστεύοντες ταῖς ἐπαγγελίαις αὐτοῦ.
2. εἶπον οἱ φύλακες τῷ ποιμένι ἵνα τηρῇ τὰ ἑπτὰ πρόβατα αὐτοῦ
παρὰ τοῖς δυσὶ ποταμοῖς. 3. μὴ μένετε ὧδε, μὴ ἴδωσιν οἱ στρατιῶται ἡμᾶς καθίζοντας παρὰ τῷ πυρί. 4. ἐλπίζετε ἐν τῷ Κυρίῳ·
μὴ εἴπητε μηδέποτε ὅτι λείψει τὸν λαὸν αὐτοῦ. 5. χαῖρε, βασιλεῦ
τῶν Ἰουδαίων· ἐκάλεσαν οἱ στρατιῶται τὸν Ἰησοῦν τούτῳ τῷ ὀνόματι (καίπερ) μὴ γινώσκοντες ὅτι λέγουσι τὴν ἀλήθειαν. 6. ὑπά-
γετε (ὕπαγε, ἀπέλθετε, ἄπελθε) ἐν εἰρήνῃ πρὸς τὴν πατρίδα (ἰδίαν
γῆν) ὑμῶν (σου)· ἐγὼ γὰρ ἐλεύσομαι (πορεύσομαι) μεθ' ὑμῶν (σὺν
ὑμῖν, μετὰ σοῦ, σὺν σοὶ) ἵνα φυλάσσω (φυλάξω) ὑμᾶς (σε).

CHAPTER 27

1. And immediately the rich man heard a voice saying: 'Fool,
this night (tonight) you must die'. 2. Watch therefore and guard
the goods of the householder (master of the house) lest a thief comes
quickly and finds you sleeping (asleep). 3. A sick man fell at the
teacher's knees and worshipped (prostrated himself) and begged
(him) to pity (have mercy, pity, compassion on) him. 4. I shall
write you a short letter lest I (in order that I may not) seem to wish
to (literally: command you many things) lay many commands
(injunctions) on you. 5. Lo! (see,) this boy's cloak is black
because the governor killed his father. 6. Whom shall we find a
faithful and true witness? For all fear (are afraid of) Caesar's
power. 7. The demoniac began to cry out and weep, for he was
not healthy (in good health), but had (literally: become) come
under the authority (power) of seven unclean demons (devils).
8. Let the foolish (fools) therefore repent immediately in order
to (that they may) receive forgiveness of sins before the hour of
death. 9. Summon all the poor and blind and lame to the wedding, for my house is not yet full. 10. We must pray therefore

that we may not enter into temptation (come to the test), for the
flesh is weak.

1. βραχεῖαί (εἰσιν) αὗται αἱ γραφαί· ἀσθενὴς γὰρ ἦν ὁ προφήτης
ὅτε ἔγραψε καὶ ἀπέστειλεν (ἐν τῷ γράψαι καὶ ἀποστεῖλαι) αὐτὰς
ταῖς ἐκκλησίαις (πρὸς τὰς ἐκκλησίας). 2. ἵνα γινώσκητε (εἰς,
πρὸς τὸ γινώσκειν) τὸ ἐμὸν εὐαγγέλιον δεῖ ὑμᾶς ἀληθῶς τηρεῖν τὰς
ἐντολάς μου ἐν ταῖς καρδίαις ὑμῶν. 3. οἱ γρηγοροῦντες δέξονται
(λήμψονται) τὸν πλήρη μισθὸν αὐτῶν μετὰ τὸ ἐλθεῖν τὸν ἄγγελον
(ἐλθόντος τοῦ ἀγγέλου) ἀπὸ τοῦ ἀμπελῶνος τοῦ κυρίου (δεσπότου)
ἡμῶν. 4. μὴ λεγέτω μηδεὶς λόγους ἄφρονας (ῥήματα ἄφρονα) ἵνα
μὴ (μὴ) ἕκαστος πείθῃ τὸν ἀδελφὸν αὐτοῦ ἁμαρτάνειν (ἁμαρτεῖν,
ἁμαρτῆσαι). 5. μὴ αἰτήσῃς (-ητε) τὸν ἰατρὸν ποιῆσαί σε ὑγιῆ
(ὑμᾶς ὑγιεῖς), ἀλλ᾽ ὁμολόγησον (-ήσατε) τὰς ἁμαρτίας σου (ὑμῶν) τῷ
Κυρίῳ ἵνα τὴν μετάνοιαν ἰδὼν (ἴδῃ καὶ) ἐλεήσῃ. 6. ἰδού, ταχέως
(ταχὺ) ἐλεύσεται ἡ ἡμέρα τοῦ Κυρίου καὶ τότε μεγάλη ἔσται ἡ
δόξα τῶν ἀληθῶν μαρτύρων ὅτι ἐμαρτύρησαν (μαρτυρησάντων, διὰ
τὸ μαρτυρῆσαι αὐτοὺς) τῇ ἑαυτῶν πίστει ἵνα εὕρωσι (εἰς, πρὸς τὸ
εὑρεῖν) ζωὴν αἰώνιον ἐν τῷ οὐρανῷ.

CHAPTER 28

1. Him who comes to me I will certainly not cast out. 2. Later
some asked (questioned) him about the parables. 3. When he
had fasted (after fasting) with the wild beasts for forty days, he was
hungry. 4. Peter was sleeping (asleep) in the prison. 5. Honour
your father and your mother in order that you may live and not
perish miserably (come to a bad end). 6. He asked the crowd to
recline on the ground and they obeyed him. 7. While the
disciples were sitting round him, he said that God loved all the
hungry and thirsty (those who were hungry and thirsty) and would
pity (have mercy, compassion on) them. 8. If you are willing
(wish), you are able to (can) heal all those who are suffering because
of disease and are sick. 9. Abraham begot Isaac. After he was
born he was willing even to kill his son when God commanded
this. 10. Who cried out in the desert? Let him be honoured

and blessed, for because of his teaching all the inhabitants of (who dwell in) Judea rejoice greatly (are exultant). 11. The king did not allow us to journey (travel) beside the sea lest we might report to the governor that he had many boats here. 12. We were unable to (could not) buy oil there in order to heal the sick, because those who heard the gospel did not believe us.

1. οἱ ἀγαπῶντες τὸν Κύριον ὄψονται αὐτὸν ἐν ταῖς ἐσχάταις ἡμέραις ἐρχόμενον ἐπὶ τῶν νεφελῶν (ταῖς νεφέλαις) ἐν δόξῃ. 2. τίς ᾔτησε (ἠρώτησε) τὸν φύλακα ἵνα ἐνέγκῃ (ἐνεγκεῖν, ἐνέγκαι) σοι (ὑμῖν) ἄρτον καὶ οἶνον ὅτε ἐπείνας (ἐπεινᾶτε) καὶ ἐδίψας (ἐδιψᾶτε) (πεινῶντι, πεινῶσι, καὶ διψῶντι, διψῶσι, ἐν τῷ πεινᾶν καὶ διψᾶν σε, ὑμᾶς); 3. οὐ δυνάμεθα οὐδὲ φαγεῖν ἄρτον ὅτι πολλοὶ ἐρωτῶσιν (πολλῶν ἐρωτώντων, διὰ τὸ ἐρωτᾶν πολλοὺς) ἡμᾶς περὶ τῶν ῥημάτων τοῦ Ἰησοῦ. 4. ὦ νεανία, βόησον ὅτι ἰάσεται (θεραπεύσει) ὁ Ἰησοῦς τοὺς ἀσθενεῖς καὶ ποιήσει αὐτοὺς ὑγιεῖς· καὶ γὰρ οὐ μὴ ἐάσῃ (ἐάσει) αὐτοὺς πάσχειν. 5. ὀφείλουσιν οἱ πιστοὶ καὶ ἅγιοι (δεῖ τοὺς πιστοὺς καὶ ἁγίους) τιμᾶν τοὺς ἄρχοντας αὐτῶν, οὓς ἀπέστειλεν ὁ Θεὸς εἰς τὸν κόσμον ἵνα ἀκούωσιν οἱ ἄνθρωποι τὰς ἐντολὰς αὐτῶν καὶ ὑπακούωσι (ἀκούοντες ὑπακούωσι, εἰς, πρὸς τὸ ἀκούειν (ἀκούσαντας) τοὺς ἀνθ. τὰς ἐντ. καὶ ὑπακούειν). 6. ἠγαλλιάσαντο οἱ ἀνακείμενοι παρὰ τῷ βασιλεῖ ἀκούσαντες (ὅτε, ὡς ἤκουσαν, ἐν τῷ ἀκούειν) ὅτι οὐκέτι ζῇ ὁ Ἰωάννης.

CHAPTER 29

1. Do not be anxious saying, What are we to drink or what are we to eat? 2. Looking round he asked them what they were saying as they journeyed, but they were silent. 3. Ought we (surely we ought not) to defile our hands and mouth by eating unclean things? 4. Does the son of man justify sinners who wrongly exalt themselves? 5. A strong man on whom no one could lay hands approached from the tombs and met him. 6. And after he had been crucified (after his crucifixion) he was manifested (appeared) to many in order that they might see and know (when they saw him they might know) that he had been raised from the dead.

7. Have not both (the) day and (the) night twelve hours? Therefore we ought to watch (keep awake) and not sleep lying down (lie
asleep). 8. Are you asking whether the teacher is departing? I
tell you that he is about to go up into the mountains and there
he will lead many astray. 9. Does not this man (he) truly liken
(compare) the kingdom of God to a man who sowed good seed in
his field? 10. Do not show yourself to the inhabitants of (those
who dwell in) the village lest the ruler rebukes me, commanding
(and commands) me to heal no longer in the name of Jesus. 11. He
is filling the city with his teaching.

1. τιμῶνται οἱ ὁρῶντες τοὺς ἀγγέλους· μεριμνᾷ γὰρ περὶ αὐτῶν ὁ
Θεός. 2. οὐχὶ δικαιοῖ ὁ Ἰησοῦς τοὺς ἀνθρώπους; μὴ οὖν πλανή-
θητε ὑπὸ τῶν ἐπιτιμώντων τοῖς πεινῶσι καὶ διψῶσιν ἁμαρτωλοῖς.
3. φανέρωσον νῦν (ἤδη) τὴν σὴν δύναμιν καὶ ἴασαι (θεράπευσον) τὴν
θυγατέρα μου, δέομαί σου· ὁ δὲ οὐκ ἠδύνατο (ἠδυνήθη). 4. ἐπετί-
μησεν ἡμῖν ὁ κύριος (δεσπότης) μὴ ὑπαντῆσαι (ἵνα μὴ ὑπαντήσωμεν)
αὐτῷ, ἐρωτῶν (ἐπερωτῶν) εἰ θέλομεν (βουλόμεθα) ἀγγεῖλαι τῷ
ἡγεμόνι ὅτι ὑπάγει (ἀπέρχεται). 5. μήτι ἐρωτᾷς (-ᾶτε) εἰ οἱ
λόγοι μου ἀληθεῖς εἰσι; 6. οὐ μεριμνῶμεν· γινώσκομεν γὰρ ὅτι ὁ
Χριστὸς ὁ ὁμοιώσας (ὃς ὡμοίωσεν) ἡμᾶς τοῖς προβάτοις αὐτοῦ
σώσει ἡμᾶς ἀπὸ (ἐκ) τῶν ἐχθρῶν ἡμῶν ἐν ἐκείνῃ τῇ ἡμέρᾳ.

CHAPTER 30

1. I am going up thither (to the place) whence (from which) I
came. 2. How can you who are evil (evil as you are) say good
things? 3. See, (literally: how many things he accuses you of) how
many accusations he brings against you! 4. We are now suffering
such tribulation as is never going to (likely to) happen later
(hereafter). 5. Many sacrifices will not help any one who denies
the son of man.* 6. But when you find that image in this country
know that the end is already near. 7. And wherever my friends
remain, there shall I remain also. 8. If you wish (are willing) to

* It is common Greek idiom to put a relative first and pick it up with a de-
monstrative which is better left untranslated.

heal this blind man, he will immediately see again. 9. We have
not such great (so much) faith as our fathers. 10. While he is
with you, you must be subject to him as having (since he has)
authority. 11. Now therefore I command (give orders to) you
that every one who does wrong (wrongdoer) be brought before the
ruler (magistrate); for he desires to judge as the governor ordered
(bade) him. 12. On the day of judgment (judgment day) the
Lord will not pity (have mercy, pity, compassion on) any one who
speaks evil against the Holy Spirit.

CHAPTER 31

1. The king has conquered (is victorious) and will come back
(return) to his native land. 2. God has made his son perfect
through sufferings. 3. Has not the ruler of this world been judged?
4. The shepherd has found the lost sheep. 5. The saints have
been (are) rooted and grounded in love. 6. The sun has become
black and we can no longer see the stars. 7. The hand of this
paralytic has been (is) withered. 8. Blessed are those who have
been persecuted on account of Christ. 9. As the patriarch Jacob
(did, like the patriarch J.) I also have married two wives and
because of this have suffered much (greatly). 10. He who trusts
in Jesus has been persuaded (is convinced) that he can save the
lost (those who have perished). 11. Lazarus has been raised from
the tomb and lives (is alive). 12. They have received the commandments, but have not been saved. 13. The Lord has granted
you this.

1. ὁ Χριστὸς ἐγηγερμένος (ἐγερθεὶς) ἐκ νεκρῶν πεφανέρωκεν ἑαυτὸν
δυσὶ γυναιξίν. 2. ὡς γέγραπται, οὐκ ἀπολεῖται (οὐ μὴ ἀπόληται)
θρὶξ (οὐδεμία) τῆς κεφαλῆς ὑμῶν (σου). 3. ποῦ εὑρήσομεν τοὺς
μεμαρτυρηκότας καὶ νῦν τεθνηκότας; 4. ἃ ἐγὼ (αὐτὸς) τεθέαμαι
καὶ ἀκήκοα (ταῦτα) κηρύξω ἐν τοῖς ἔθνεσιν. 5. ἰδού, τεθεράπευται
(ἴαται, differentiated by accent from present ἰᾶται) ἡ χεὶρ ἡ
ἐξηραμμένη. 6. τὰ σπέρματα τὰ ἐπὶ γῆν κακὴν ἐσπαρμένα (ἃ
ἔσπαρται, ἐσπαρμένα εἰσί) οὐ φέρει (φέρουσι) καρπόν.

CHAPTER 32

1. When did you come? Once upon a time there was (was born, came, arose) a great prophet. Where is your (sing.) house? Whence did you learn this? (Where . . . from?) I wrote this somewhere. How many loaves have you? Why did you (sing.) do this? How have you fear? (how is it that you are afraid?) What kind of teaching is this? 2. Before Jesus appeared a great crowd had come together. 3. But he knowing their hypocrisy said to them, Why do you tempt me? (put me to the test?) 4. No one knew that this man (he) was the Messiah (Christ). 5. We have beheld signs (miracles) that have happened through the name of Jesus and now we shall be believers (believe) in him. 6. John was clothed with (used to wear) camel's hair. 7. For John used to say to Herod, It is not lawful for you to have your brother's wife. 8. Those therefore who have been sealed by baptism ought to walk in the way of the Lord not denying (and not deny) his commandments. 9. The women have seen a young man sitting on the right wearing a white robe. 10. Surely the magi (wise men) have not told Herod that they have found the little child (for) whom they were seeking? 11. Are you not blaspheming, saying (when you say) that this man cast out demons only through the devil? 12. As he was accustomed (as was his habit, custom) he went up to the mountain and was alone there praying. 13. In order that you may all know the truth I will tell you that after his resurrection he went up into heaven.

1. ὡς εἴρηται ὑπυ τοῦ προφήτου, Οὐ δύναται ἐκ τοῦ τόπου τούτου οὐδὲν ἀγαθὸν ἐλθεῖν. 2. ἐληλύθασιν ἄρτι πολλοὶ στρατιῶται ἵνα νικήσωσι (νικῆσαι, εἰς, πρὸς τὸ νικῆσαι) τοὺς ἐχθροὺς ταχέως (ταχὺ) πρὸ τοῦ δύνασθαι αὐτοὺς φυγεῖν. 3. ὅστις ἂν εἰδῇ ὅτι οὕτως ἐδίδαξεν ὁ Χριστός (διδάξαι, διδάξαντα τὸν Χριστόν), οὗτος ὀφείλει (τοῦτον δεῖ) πέμπειν ἀργύριον τοῖς τελώναις (πρὸς τοὺς τελώνας). 4. κατέκειτο (βεβλημένη ἦν) ἡ γυνὴ ἐπὶ τὴν κλίνην (τῆς κλίνης, τῇ κλίνῃ) καὶ ἐξεληλύθει (-εισαν) ἐξ αὐτῆς τὰ ἑπτὰ δαιμόνια. 5. οὐχὶ οἴδατε (ἴστε, οἶδας) ἐν τίνι (ποίᾳ) ἐξουσίᾳ ἐκήρυξε τὸ εὐαγγέλιον (εὐηγγελίσατο); 6. ὡς γέγραπται ἐν τούτῳ τῷ βιβλίῳ, ἐλεήσω τὸν λαόν μου καὶ οὐκέτι μνησθήσομαι τῶν ἁμαρτιῶν αὐτῶν.

CHAPTER 33

1. Leaving the (their) nets in the boat they (they left . . . and) followed him. 2. Lo! he who betrays me (my betrayer) has drawn near (i.e. is at hand, near). 3. Then the apostles laid their hands upon them and prayed that the Lord would give these (them) also a part (share) of the Holy Spirit. 4. The saints give their wealth to those who have need. 5. And it came to pass, on that day the Lord added many to the multitude of the believers. 6. Immediately therefore he ordered them to set the five loaves and two fishes before the multitude because they were all hungry and had come (gathered) together from the city. 7. How much wage did you pay to those last workmen? 8. He thought that his brothers understood that through his hand (by his agency) God was giving them salvation (deliverance), but they did not understand. 9. Do you know that when he sent Jesus into the world God changed the law? 10. Surely you have not given all the scriptures to the soldiers to be destroyed? 11. What sort of wine will you give us when my son marries your daughter? 12. The prophets used to hand down wise and sound sayings to those who wished (were willing) to hear. 13. He looked at him and loved him and said to him, Go, sell (literally: as many things as, τοσαῦτα understood) all that you have and give to the poor. 14. I do not understand yet.

1. μετὰ τὸ θεῖναι (θεὶς) τὸν νεκρὸν ἐν τῷ μνημείῳ ἀπῆλθε (ὑπήγαγε). 2. διδότω ὁ ἀγαπῶν τὸν Θεὸν ἄρτον τοῖς πεινῶσι. 3. μεταδώσεις τὴν σὴν δύναμίν μοι; 4. δεῖ σε (ὑμᾶς, ὀφείλεις, ὀφείλετε) ἀποδιδόναι (-δοῦναι) μισθὸν (μισθοὺς) τοῖς ὑπηρέταις καὶ μὴ (μηδὲ, not οὐ, because it governs the infin.) προστιθέναι (-θεῖναι) τῷ σῷ (ὑμετέρῳ) πλούτῳ. 5. μόνος (μόνον) ὁ Θεὸς δύναται ἀφιέναι (ἀφεῖναι) (τὰς) ἁμαρτίας. 6. παρέδομεν (-εδώκαμεν) τοῖς τέκνοις ἡμῶν τὸ εὐαγγέλιον ὃ ἐδεξάμεθα (ἐλάβομεν) ἵνα ἀκούωσι (ἀκούσωσι) (εἰς, πρὸς τὸ ἀκούειν, ἀκοῦσαι, αὐτοὺς) τοὺς λόγους τῆς αἰωνίου ζωῆς.

CHAPTER 34

1. You (sing.) have announced. He (she, it) has been judged. You (pl.) have heard. It has been said. He (she, it) has been hidden. Having been raised. He (she, it) had come. He (she, it) has been crucified. 2. This man (he) was so strong that no one was able to (could) plunder his goods. 3. For how much did you sell the field? 4. Let us therefore lay aside the works of darkness and put on the weapons (armour) of light. 5. The Lord covenanted (appointed, made) this new covenant for (with) the people. 6. They therefore entrusted their friends to the Lord having prayed (after praying) that he would always guard them so as to fear nothing. 7. When they heard Peter's words many were added to the church so that the crowd was amazed and said, Never have we seen such things. 8. And he gave authority to the disciples (so as) to do (perform) many signs and wonders. 9. For I tell you that authority has been given me (so as) to forgive men sins. 10. Therefore the owner will let out the vineyard to others. 11. Now because I know that you are righteous I exhort (urge) you to come and lay your hands on my sick slave and heal him. 12. But if anyone blasphemes against the Holy Spirit, the sin will not be forgiven him, not even if he repents with all his heart (wholeheartedly).

1. τὸ ἀργύριον τοῦτο ὃ ἡρπάγη (τὸ ἁρπαγὲν) ὑπὸ τῶν λῃστῶν προστεθήσεται τῷ πλούτῳ τῶν πλουσίων, ἀλλ' οὐδὲν δέδοται τοῖς πτωχοῖς. 2. ἐδίδου ὁ πατήρ μου ἄρτον καὶ ὕδωρ τοῖς ἐν φυλακῇ πεινῶσι καὶ διψῶσιν. 3. ἀπέδοτο οὖν τὸν οἶκον ἑαυτοῦ καὶ ἔθηκε τὸ ἀργύριον παρὰ τοὺς πόδας (cf. Acts 5.35) τῶν ἀποστόλων ὥστε ὠφελεῖν τὰς χήρας. 4. ἀφέωνται ὑμῖν πᾶσαι αἱ ἁμαρτίαι ὅτι συνίετε ταῦτα τὰ ῥήματα καὶ δέχεσθε (λαμβάνετε) ἐν ταῖς καρδίαις ὑμῶν (διὰ τὸ συνιέναι καὶ δέχεσθαι, λαμβάνειν, συνιεῖσι . . . καὶ δεχομένοις, λαμβάνουσι, participle to agree with ὑμῖν). 5. μετὰ τὸ παραδοθῆναι τὸν Ἰησοῦν (παραδοθεὶς ὁ Ἰησοῦς) ἤχθη ὑπὸ τῶν φυλάκων ἔμπροσθεν (ἐπὶ) τοῦ ἀρχιερέως. 6. οὕτως καλὴ γέγονεν (γεγένηται) αὕτη ἡ παρθένος ὥστε πάντας τοὺς ἄνδρας θεωροῦντας (θεωμένους, ὅταν θεωρῶσι, θεῶνται) αὐτὴν θέλειν (βούλεσθαι, ἐπιθυμεῖν) γαμῆσαι.

δίδωσι 3rd sing. present indic. active of
   δίδωμι δώσω ἔδωκα δέδωκα δέδομαι ἐδόθην *give*
ἐπέθηκε 3rd sing. aorist indic. active of
   ἐπιτίθημι   ἐπιθήσω   ἐπέθηκα   ἐπιτέθεικα   ἐπιτέθειμαι
   ἐπετέθην *lay on*
ἤφιε 3rd sing. imperfect indic. active of ἀφίω
   ἀφίημι ἀφήσω ἀφῆκα ἀφεῖκα ἀφεῖμαι ἀφέθην *remit*
προσετέθησαν 3rd pl. aorist indic. passive, meaning *add*
συνῆκαν 3rd pl. aorist indic. active, meaning *understand*
παραθῶμεν 1st pl. aorist subj. active, meaning *set before*
ἀπέδοσθε 2nd pl. aorist indic. middle, meaning *sell*
ἀφεθήσεται 3rd sing. fut. indic. passive, meaning *remit*
For the principal parts of these last five see the forms given above.

1. And immediately one of those standing by (the bystanders) asked him (saying), Do not you also follow this man? (Are not you also a follower of this man?)   2. He rose and went up into the temple in order to present (offer) a sacrifice there to God.   3. When are you going to restore the kingdom to Israel?   4. We cannot stand against (withstand, resist) the evil one (*or*, if taken as the neuter, evil) if God does not help us (unless God helps us).   5. All the scribes were amazed at his wisdom.   6. Today I am standing before the judge, so that (with the result that) my enemies are rejoicing.   7. Paul constituted (appointed) elders in each city and kneeling entrusted them to the Lord.   8. After he had suffered (after his passion) he presented himself alive to the disciples. 9. But he denied (it) saying, I neither know nor understand what you are saying (mean).   10. He said to him, Stand up on your feet.   And he, recognizing (realizing) that he could stand and walk, rejoiced and blessed God who had taken pity on him.   11. Fools ought not to be constituted (appointed) (as) rulers (It is not fools who . . ., bringing out emphasis of μέν), but just (righteous) men who know how to do (act) justly (righteously).   12. Some bandits immediately came upon him and plundered his belongings and

left him in the desert that the wild beasts might eat him (for the wild beasts to eat). 13. For the son of man came to give his soul (i.e. life) (as) a ransom for many. 14. For this I understand (know) well, that my withered (paralysed) hand was restored.

1. καὶ ἀναστὰς παρέθηκε τὸ πρόβατον τῷ ποιμένι (ἔθηκεν . . . ἔμπροσθεν τοῦ ποιμένος). 2. οὐ στησόμεθα (σταθησόμεθα) ἔμπροσθεν αὐτοῦ ὅταν ἔλθῃ ἐν τῇ δόξῃ τῶν ἀγγέλων αὐτοῦ· πάντες (ἅπαντες) γὰρ παραδεδώκαμεν αὐτόν. 3. ἔστησεν ὁ φύλαξ τὸν προφήτην ἐν μέσῳ τῶν στρατιωτῶν καὶ ἐκέλευσε τοὺς ἄλλους (παρήγγειλε, προσέταξε, ἐνετείλατο τοῖς ἄλλοις) ἀποστῆναι (ἵνα ἀποστῶσιν) ἀπ᾽ αὐτοῦ. 4. ἐποιήθη (ἐποιήθησαν) πολλὰ σημεῖα καὶ τέρατα ἐν ἐκείνῃ τῇ πόλει ὥστε ἐξίστασθαι (ἐκπλήσσεσθαι) τὸν ὄχλον (τὸ πλῆθος) ἐπὶ τῇ δυνάμει τῶν ἀποστόλων. 5. ὁ ἄγγελος ὁ ἑστηκὼς (ἑστὼς) ἔμπροσθεν τοῦ Θεοῦ λέγει αὐτῷ περὶ τῶν ἀνθρώπων· ὁ δὲ ἀφήσει αὐτοῖς τὰς ἁμαρτίας. 6. εἱστήκεισαν (εἱστήκει) ἔξω τὰ τέκνα λέγοντα (οἱ παῖδες λέγοντες) ὅτι πεινῶσι καὶ διψῶσιν.

CHAPTER 36

ἀναστάς nom. sing. m. 2nd aorist participle active of

ἀνίστημι ἀναστήσω $\begin{cases} ἀνέστησα \\ ἀνέστην \end{cases}$ ἀνέστηκα ἀνέσταμαι ἀνεστάθην

raise up

σβέννυται 3rd sing. present indic. middle and passive of
σβέννυμι σβέσω ἔσβεσα quench

ἑστάναι perfect infin. active of ἵστημι cause to stand
perfect active used intransitively with present meaning stand.
For principal parts see above under ἀνίστημι.

ἀποκαθιστάνεις 2nd sing. present indic. active of ἀποκαθιστάνω
restore
For principal parts see above under ἀνίστημι.

δεῖξον 2nd sing. aorist imperative active of
δείκνυμι δείξω ἔδειξα δέδειχα δέδειγμαι ἐδείχθην show

ἐπιγνοῦσα nom. sing. fem. aorist participle active of
   ἐπιγινώσκω   ἐπιγνώσομαι   ἐπέγνων   ἐπέγνωκα   ἐπέγνωσμαι
   ἐπεγνώσθην recognize
ἀπολωλός nom. and acc. sing. neuter perfect participle active of
   ἀπόλλυμι   ἀπολῶ   ἀπώλεσα   destroy
              ἀπολοῦμαι ἀπωλόμην ἀπόλωλα perish
δείκνυσι 3rd sing. present indic. active of δείκνυμι show
   For principal parts see above.

1. The high priests and scribes were seeking how they might (a means to) seize (arrest) Jesus and destroy him, but not in (during) the festival. 2. The lamps are being quenched (going out) because we did not buy oil. 3. Those who stood by (the bystanders) began to rail and swear, saying, This man wants to destroy our people. 4. The angel who is called Abaddon among the Jews is named Apollyon (Destroyer) in the Greek tongue. 5. And I swore in my wrath that they should certainly not enter this country. 6. Therefore one man who has done nothing worthy of death must perish on behalf of many, lest the Romans fearing (fear and, because of fear) hate us. 7. He who (literally: works righteousness) does righteous works (acts righteously) shows the commandments inscribed in (on) his heart. 8. When he had given thanks he ordered the men to recline in order that the disciples might set bread before them. 9. The kingdom of heaven is like a woman who lost a silver coin (piece of silver) and when she had found the lost (coin) (what she had lost) she rejoiced. 10. And he said, The Lord will not allow us to be tempted (tried) beyond what we can (bear) (our strength). For before the devil destroys us he will come to save. 11. The king clothes his children (boys, sons) in such a way that the crowds are amazed when they see these beautiful clothes. 12. Now I exhort you, show me your hands and feet in order that I may believe that you rose from the dead after being crucified (you were crucified, your crucifixion). 13. When Peter laid on (imposed) his hands even (the) little children were filled with Holy Spirit. 14. Never swear.

1. πρὶν (πρὸ τοῦ) συλλαβεῖν τοὺς στρατιώτας τὸν Ἰησοῦν ὠμόσατε ὅτι οὐ μὴ ἀπαρνήσησθε (ἀπαρνήσεσθε) αὐτόν. 2. ἐὰν ἀκολουθήσητε τούτῳ δείξει ὑμῖν μέγαν οἶκον οὗ (ὅπου) δεῖ (ὑμᾶς) ἑτοιμάσαι εἰς

35

τὴν ἑορτήν. 3. ἐργάσεται ὁ ἀπόστολος πολλὰ σημεῖα καὶ τέρατα οὕτως δεικνὺς τὴν ἀληθῆ δύναμιν τοῦ Θεοῦ. 4. πλανᾶται (πλα-νῶνται) τὰ ἀπολωλότα πρόβατα ἐπὶ τὸ ὄρος (τοῦ ὄρους, τῷ ὄρει)· ἀπῆλθε (ὑπήγαγε) γὰρ ὁ πονηρὸς ποιμὴν πρὶν (πρὸ τοῦ) εὑρεῖν αὐτά· 5. καὶ ὤμοσας ἐν τῇ ὀργῇ σου λέγων, Ἀπολοῦνται πάντες οἱ μισοῦντες (οἳ μισοῦσι) τὰ ἀγαθὰ (καλὰ) ἔργα. 6. καὶ ἀναστὰς ἐζώσατο (cf. Acts 12.8) καὶ ἐξῆλθεν ὑπαντῆσαι (ἵνα ὑπαντήσῃ, εἰς, πρὸς τὸ ὑπαντῆσαι) τῷ κυρίῳ (δεσπότῃ) αὐτοῦ.

CHAPTER 37

1. These virgins (girls) are wiser than those foolish ones, for they have oil in their lamps so as to be able to meet the bridegroom quickly. 2. Among all let marriage be most holy so that no one may (literally: stand away from) divorce his own wife. 3. This scribe has written more accurately than all those who tried to make (compose) a treatise (cf. Acts 1.1) about (concerning) this time. 4. Those other witnesses loved (the) truth more than life. 5. In that temple lie (have been placed) vessels of most precious (valu-able) wood. 6. And it came to pass, after the children approached (drew) nearer, Jesus wished to lay his hands on their heads in order that he might (to) bless them. 7. But whoever is willing to keep the weightier commandments of the law, O most excellent Theo-philus, will keep the least also. 8. Therefore the worse (baser) citizens were crying out, though they knew very well that you had not sinned, saying, He must be crucified very quickly (with all speed). 9. But the Highest who makes (produces) fruit for men gives no less to the bad than to the good. 10. Therefore none of your limbs will become (be) excessive (superfluous), for the body is constituted from (them) all. 11. I shall talk to you more speedily (sooner) if I can, for journeying further than I was about to do (intended) I hope to come very near (you). 12. And he asked, Which is easier, to take up your cross and follow me or to eat and drink (literally: remaining most enjoyably) and enjoy yourselves remaining with the Gentiles? 13. Men shall see greater things than these in the last days when the son of man comes to judge the world well and carefully.

1. δεῖ τοὺς τελειοτέρους (ὀφείλουσιν οἱ τελειότεροι) ὠφελεῖν τοὺς ἀσθενεστέρους ἀδελφούς. 2. σοφώτερός ἐστιν ὁ Θεὸς τῶν ἀνθρώπων (ἢ οἱ ἄνθρωποι)· εὖ (κάλλιον) γὰρ οἶδε (γινώσκει) (διὰ) τί ἧσσον τίμιοί εἰσι τῶν ἀγγέλων (ἢ οἱ ἄγγελοι). 3. καινοτέρα ἐστὶν αὕτη ἡ διαθήκη ἐκείνης (ἢ ἐκείνη)· θέλει (βούλεται) γὰρ ὁ Θεὸς δοῦναι ἑτέραν καὶ κρείσσονα (κρείσσω) ἐλπίδα τοῖς ἀνθρώποις. 4. χείρων καλεῖται αὕτη ἡ ἁμαρτία ὅτι πάντες γινώσκουσι (οἴδασι, πάντων γινωσκόντων, εἰδότων, διὰ τὸ γινώσκειν, εἰδέναι πάντας) ὅτι οἱ μισοῦντες τοὺς ἀδελφοὺς ἑαυτῶν οὐκ ἄξιοί εἰσι (τοὺς μισοῦντας . . . οὐκ ἀξίους εἶναι, ὄντας) τῆς ἀφέσεως ἣν δίδωσιν ὁ Θεὸς διὰ τοῦ ἰδίου υἱοῦ. 5. γέγονεν (γεγένηται) ὁ Χριστὸς ὑψηλότερος τῶν ἀγγέλων (ἢ οἱ ἄγγελοι)· μείζονα (μείζω) γὰρ ἔχει δόξαν καὶ κρεῖσσον ὄνομα. 6. ὃ ἔχεις (ἔχετε) περισσοτέρως (περισσότερον) δεῖ μεταδιδόναι (μεταδοῦναι) τοῖς πτωχοῖς οἳ ἧσσον ἔχουσιν ἢ σύ (ὑμεῖς). 7. οἱ πλεῖστον ἀργύριον σώζοντες γίνονται πλούσιοι, οἱ δὲ δίκαιοι δέξονται (λήμψονται) μείζονα (μείζω) μισθὸν ἐν τῇ βασιλείᾳ τοῦ οὐρανοῦ (τῶν οὐρανῶν).

CHAPTER 38

1. After the festival about the first hour they stood in the presence of (before) the governor. 2. I was sleeping by the lake and in a dream I seemed to see somebody walking on the water. 3. These men have said nothing against the temple nor do they persuade us contrary to law not to accept (to stop accepting) the commandments which have been handed down to us from the (our) fathers. 4. He said, Because of your righteousness you shall be saved and shall receive power from God (so as) to answer the (your) judges. 5. He shall always stand over (be in charge of) my house so that (in order that) he may give a more accurate account about my belongings to the tax-collectors. 6. All the bystanders were amazed at this new teaching. 7. When I saw you under the tree I knew that you were a man according to (after) my own heart. 8. And now instead of the old promises you have received new grace. 9. This girl (maiden) therefore who found favour with the Lord bore a son in due season. 10. In the time of this prophet

37

many died for their native land resisting the enemy. 11. You have suffered many things (much), but the Lord will not try you beyond what you can (bear) (your strength). 12. I tell you that I will give you five denarii (coins) apiece if you (will) go to the vineyard and work with the rest who have already been sent forth (despatched).

CHAPTER 39

Around the throne. Down from the mountain. With the angel (messenger). Through the land. He used to live in the time of Herod. He is lodging at Peter's (house). He is wiser than his brothers. He was crucified on a gibbet (tree). They were astonished at his teaching.

1. The blind man when he received his sight reported in (throughout) the city what great things Jesus had done for him. 2. But whoever does not reverence (feels no respect for) his friends is going to (is likely to) disregard you too. 3. And he permitted the demons to enter the swine. 4. Leaving their nets in the boat they went along with Jesus. 5. For those who expect the kingdom of heaven must endure the things that happen (what befalls) on account of their faith. 6. The attendants set good wine before those who were reclining (at table, dining) with the governor, but inferior wine before the others. 7. They departed to their own country without revealing (and did not reveal) this to the king. 8. When he had taken down the body he placed it in a new tomb. 9. Those who had been invited to the wedding all began to excuse themselves. 10. When he had removed (on removing) from the village he was killed by those who already wished to destroy his authority. 11. While the eunuch was reading the book, lo! Philip immediately came upon him. 12. But when the corpse came to life again all those passing by (the passers by), knowing that Jesus had raised him, rejoiced with the mother and lifted up their voice giving thanks to God.

θαλάσσης θαλάσσαις ἡ lake (sea)   δεσπότου δεσπόταις ὁ master
αἰῶνος αἰῶσι(ν) ὁ age   φύλακος φύλαξι(ν) ὁ guard
λαμπάδος λαμπάσι(ν) ἡ lamp   γυναικός γυναιξί(ν) ἡ woman
πατρός πατράσι(ν) ὁ father   ποδός ποσί(ν) ὁ foot
χειρός χερσί(ν) ἡ hand   σώματος σώμασι(ν) τό body

1. My little daughter was ten years old and so much wiser than all her friends that many men wished to converse with her because of this. 2. He said that they stole your money by night, deposited it in a little boat and carried it away across the sea outside our borders (territory). 3. Having fasted (after fasting, when we had fasted) five days we were standing in front of the priest and reported to him that we had completed without sin all that he commanded us (all his commands). 4. But under the table many little dogs which belong (belonging) to the master of the house eat bread. 5. When they arrived near the city running after the soldiers they gladly lay down on the ground opposite the river. 6. The heart of the wicked is far distant from the Lord, but what is within them (the inside) will be made manifest on the day of judgment. 7. Woman, such transgressions will be forgiven, for these your neighbours (of yours) are much worse who do not confess that they sinned before God. 8. John used to baptize with water, but all the disciples except Judas who betrayed Jesus were baptized with fire. 9. I was lying all night on (on top of) a mattress between two attendants. 10. In body I am weak, but in soul stronger (or very strong) because of faith in Jesus.

1. ἀπεχόμεθα (τοῦ) οἴνου (ἐν) ταύτῃ τῇ ἡμέρᾳ ἕνεκα τῶν ἀσθενῶν (τῶν ἀσθ. χάριν). 2. τρία ἔτη κατῴκουν κατέναντι τούτου τοῦ ὄρους ἵνα ὦ (εἰς, πρὸς τὸ εἶναι) ἐγγὺς τῆς μητρός μου. 3. πέραν τοῦ ποταμοῦ εὑρήσεις (εὑρήσετε) δούλους τινὰς ἑστῶτας ἔξω τῆς πόλεως. 4. ὄμνυμι ἐνώπιον (ἔμπροσθεν) τοῦ Θεοῦ ὅτι ἠγόρασα ταῦτα τὰ πρόβατα πολλοῦ ἀργυρίου. 5. ἀπέχει ὁ πλούσιος τὸν ἴδιον μισθόν· πλήν, οὗτος ὁ πτωχὸς ὀνόματι Λάζαρος ἀντὶ θλίψεως ἕξει πολλὴν χαρὰν ἐν τῷ οὐρανῷ.

CHAPTER 41

1. If I were still pleasing men I would not be a slave of Christ.
2. If (ever) your brother sins, rebuke him and if he repents forgive him. 3. If you give heed to those who both lie and blaspheme, know that the rest will no longer believe (trust) you. 4. If (ever) a man divorces his wife except for (on the grounds of) fornication he will be condemned before God. 5. If you loved those who grieve and hate you, you would not be paying them back (rendering) evil for evil. 6. If any man seems (is reputed) wise among you in this age, let him become a fool in order that he may become wise. 7. You know neither me nor my Father. For if you knew me, you would know my Father also. 8. If anyone has not the Spirit of Christ, he is not his. 9. If (ever) anyone grieves his brother, he ought to repent immediately, lest he grieves the Holy Spirit. 10. For if they had known they would not have crucified the Lord of glory. 11. If I had not been present on that day I should not have seen the crowds running towards Jesus. 12. If we had not toiled throughout the night we would neither have taken so many fish nor would we now have them for supper.

1. ἐὰν λαλῶσι γλώσσαις τινὲς οὐ δεῖ λέγειν αὐτοὺς (οὐκ ὀφείλουσι λέγειν) ὅτι σοφώτεροί εἰσι (σοφωτέρους εἶναι ἑαυτοὺς) τῶν λοιπῶν ἀδελφῶν (ἢ οἱ λοιποὶ ἀδελφοί, ὑπὲρ, παρὰ τοὺς λοιποὺς ἀδελφούς).
2. ἐὰν μὴ ἴδητε σημεῖα καὶ τέρατα οὐ μὴ πιστεύσητε (πιστεύσετε).
3. εἰ τοῦτο εἶπεν ὁ τυφλὸς μάρτυς ἐψεύσατο τῷ πλουσίῳ κριτῇ.
4. ἐὰν ἐπιτρέψῃ (ἀφῇ) ἡμῖν (ἐάσῃ ἡμᾶς) ὁ ἡγεμὼν τηρῆσαι (τηρεῖν) τοῦτο τὸ ἀργύριον δώσομεν αὐτὸ τῇ πτωχῇ χήρᾳ. 5. εἰ ἀνέγνως (ἀνέγνωτε) τὰς γραφὰς εὗρες (εὕρετε) ἂν τοὺς λόγους τούτους.
6. εἰ ἁμαρτωλὸς ἦν οὐκ ἂν ἐξέβαλλε (τὰ) δαιμόνια.

CHAPTER 42

1. And Mary said, Behold, the handmaid of the Lord; be it unto me according to thy word. (Luke 1.38 RV.) 2. Peter said to him, (literally: may your money be along with you unto destruction)

Your silver perish with you. (Acts 8.20 RSV.) 3. And they asked the father what he would like the baby to be called. 4. May the God of peace himself sanctify you and may your spirit and soul and body be kept (literally: blamelessly) without blame at the coming of our Lord Jesus Christ (cf. I Thess. 5.23). 5. Accordingly I enquired whether he wished to travel to Jerusalem. 6. When the blind man heard the crowd passing through he enquired what this was (might be). 7. No one took my part; all deserted me. May it not be charged against them! (RSV) (May it not be laid to their account. RV) II Tim. 4.16. 8. The twelve were considering which might be the greatest of them. 9. Are we to sin because we are not under law but under grace? God forbid. (RV) (By no means! RSV) (Of course not. NEB) Rom. 6.15. 10. Now the God of peace, who brought again from the dead the great shepherd of the sheep with the blood of the eternal covenant, (even) our Lord Jesus, make you perfect in every good thing to do his will. (Heb. 13.20, 21 RV.)

CHAPTER 43

1. I am not fit that the Lord should grant me mercy. 2. Thus he will come upon the clouds in the way in which you beheld him going into heaven (the sky). 3. He used to sit daily at the door of the temple in order to ask alms from those who were going in (entered). 4. Grant us that we may sit near you when your kingdom comes. 5. When we had met together and heard these things (this), both we and the rest exhorted (urged) him not to go away. 6. For the king was about to (intended to) seek (search) for the child (baby) in order to destroy him. 7. But the crowds were trying to restrain him from departing (leaving). 8. Therefore if you desire to be saved reject nothing of what the prophets have handed down to you (no part of the prophetic tradition). 9. It is expedient that the passover should be sacrificed in that month. 10. Jesus said (that) he was unwilling that the disciples should (continue to) prevent the little children from coming to him. 11. Until the day on which the Lord was taken up (ascended) the

disciples were ignorant (did not know) that they must preach the gospel throughout the whole world. 12. Why do you gaze at us as if by our own power we have made him walk? (cf. Acts 5.12).

CHAPTER 44

1. The young (new) heir therefore will inherit three vineyards, each (one) containing 70 trees apiece. 2. But the 6th workman was unwilling (refused) to work so as to receive only a small wage daily (for only a small daily wage). 3. Of the free men 4,000 were killed in that war, but of the slaves 7,699. 4. The 7th girl (possessive dative) has neither silver nor gold (cf. Acts 3.6). However 11 wish to marry her because she is beautiful and good. 5. But the younger of the two shepherds was considering in himself (thinking to himself), saying, What shall I do? (am I to do?) For 87 sheep are straying (astray) nor, though I have often sought, can I (and . . . I cannot) find the lost. 6. On the third day he rose from the dead and appeared to above (more than) 500 brothers. 7. But on the fiftieth day (at Pentecost) about (literally: as if) 120 brothers were gathered together at Jerusalem. 8. This man (he) wishes that we should (us to) buy 6 loaves for 3 denarii (in order) to set before these 8 widows. 9. The 10,000 saints cried out with a loud voice blessing God. 10. They brought 1,000 prisoners to Damascus, 400 of whom they left there and 500 they handed over to the king and 100 they killed immediately. 11. Three times therefore I (they) (literally: kept on bringing) offered both gold and brass, but the ruler was unwilling to accept lest perhaps somebody might say that he was about to judge unjustly (was likely to give an unjust verdict) because he had been persuaded by gifts (bribed). 12. The twelfth who betrayed Christ is dead. Therefore (so) we the remaining 11 must choose one witness of the resurrection.